The Strike That Changed
Maryland's Wilderness County

Len Shindel

The Strike That Changed Maryland's Wilderness County
By Len Shindel
Copyright © 2025 by Len Shindel

Library of Congress Cataloging-in-Publication Data:
Shindel, Len

1. Garrett County 2. Working class literature 3. Garrett County Road Workers 4. Labor Union 5. Maryland History 6. Public Sector Workers

Cover art and all photos not otherwise credited courtesy of the AFSCME Archives-Walter P. Reuther Library, Wayne State University.

ISBN: 979-8-9898025-6-2

Book design & formatting by Matthew Tallon

For information about the book and to request copies, email: hardballpress@gmail.com

DEDICATION

We dedicate this book to:

- Mountain Maryland's working families in the hope we may know and appreciate the hidden history and sacrifices of those who came and struggled before us.
- The men and women from so many corners of Garrett County and far beyond who took the time to tell their stories about the Garrett County Road Worker Strike of 1970.
- All who supported the strike's commemoration with a historic road marker, encouraging others to similarly honor their counties' histories of working-class struggle.
- The strikers from Friendsville to Red House, members of American Federation of State County and Municipal Employees (AFSCME) Local 1834, who maintained nearly 700 miles of county roads and opened new ground for public workers everywhere.

TABLE OF CONTENTS

FORWARD

The book you are about to read is the product of extensive interviews with Garrett County residents on both sides of the 1970 strike. Where quotes are not attributed to other sources, they are from those interviews and discussions—in person, by phone or e-mail—conducted between 2019 and 2024 with former commissioner John "Ross" Sines, strikers, their families, and many others.

The book details a historic conflict between residents of Garrett County. That battle took place in a region that was diverse and complex.

The 48 miles between Cumberland—once Maryland's second-largest city—and Oakland was a passage from a raucous, union-dense manufacturing market to a less contentious, more conservative farm and extraction-based economy.

While Cumberland had a racially diverse working class, Garrett County's Oakland was and remains overwhelmingly white. Historic sources and more contemporary interviews in this book often reflect language flowing from the racial homogeneity and insularity of Garrett County. I have tried to maintain historical accuracy and authenticity while being sensitive to important changes in today's language and understanding of race and class.

When I left Baltimore County in 2015 and retired full-time to Mountain Maryland, I had scant knowledge of my bountiful new county's history and the regional nuances that affected its economics, culture and politics

I had, however, spent forty-two years in the labor movement, giving me an appreciation for that element of the regional economy. For 31 years I worked at Bethlehem Steel's Sparrows Point, Maryland plant, serving in numerous elected positions in Steelworkers Local 2609 and 9477. During the final 11 years of my career, I worked as a media specialist in the Washington, D.C. headquarters of the International Brotherhood of Electrical Workers.

Labor history was always one of my passions. Even before I moved to Garrett County, I had heard about the 1970 Garrett County Road Department Strike. Intent upon getting some of the real dirt and gravel on the 1970 strike, one day I drove to the Garrett County Historical Society Museum in Oakland. I asked the volunteer at the desk what materials they had on the road worker strike. Her search through the file cabinets and the index of *The Glades Star*, the society's magazine, came up empty.

I thanked her and walked up Main Street to the Ruth Enlow Library (the public library of Oakland), past the tidy replica of the long-gone, plush, and expansive Deer Park Hotel, once perched nearby, where U.S. presidents vacationed.

Across from the replica stands the spectacular B&O station where the servants of U.S. presidents unloaded luggage. I walked past St. Matthew's Episcopal Church, where the presidents prayed, built by the B&O's CEO John W. Garrett. I noted the steeple that rang out for a paint job and the rector who on Saturdays sold his Country Parson Honey at the farmer's market just beyond the train station on the Little Youghiogheny River.

The farmer's market is the most diverse setting in this slot of Maryland, wedged between West Virginia and Pennsylvania. It's the turf where Mennonite couples in bib overalls and white kapps (bonnets) sell their baked bread and carrots alongside men in tie-dyed shirts and young women in old granny skirts who peddle kale and mushrooms. Some of the men in both tribes sport beards that appear to have never felt the bristles of a brush. People of color are rarely present, a stark difference from my life in Baltimore.

At the library, a friendly and helpful librarian began threading a microfilm spool of 1970 editions of *The Republican* newspaper. Founded in 1877, *The Republican* is a treasure to any Garrett County historian, as well as many a returning wayfarer looking for Uncle Jimmy's war story or great grandmother's obituary.

Hooked on the headlines and enthralled by the stories of the strike, I needed to know more. The road workers of Garrett County, who maintain 700 miles of asphalt and gravel, build fine bridges and plow the deepest snows in Maryland had a right to their history side-by-side with the presidents and first ladies in the county museum.

Getting their stories wasn't always easy. I didn't have phone numbers for many, just a location along a stream or a stretch of farmland. One man said he was sworn to secrecy about how AFSCME came on the scene and didn't want anyone to know I had spoken with him. A couple of strikers said they'd give me five minutes to talk about eight hard months.

I needed some help.

Garrett County is a place where a 104-year-old, well-known businessman dies and his obituary in *The Republican* says he wasn't a "native" because he was brought here at age six months by parents from "outside." How would I, a most legitimate outsider raised by Jewish liberals, convince these folks to tell me their stories?

A remarkable turn of events gave me the leverage to extend some of the strikers' five minutes into hours. One of my co-workers in the steel mill was the great nephew of Ross Sines. Sines, 38 at the time of the strike, was the county commissioner who led opposition to recognizing AFSCME Local 1834. Now 91, he lived 15 minutes from our new home in Garrett County.

Like so many local families, including most of the strikers I spoke with, some of Ross Sines' kin had left the county's farming, logging, coal mining and railroad work behind and moved to Baltimore for more stable industrial jobs.

I called Sines' nephew, told him about my project and asked if he could help get me an interview with Ross. Josh spoke to his father and his uncle. They declined, worried that reliving the experience might be too fraught with emotion for an old man.

But a week later, Sines' nephew called back and said Ross Sines wanted to talk. He let Sines know I was "one-hundred-percent union," but he told his great uncle I could be trusted to accurately tell his side of the story.

Ross Sines and his wife Marie were extremely gracious with their time and detail. There couldn't be a deeper or wider chasm between me, a suburban-raised veteran of the anti-war movement of the late 60s, and a Christian fundamentalist farmer who says higher education is the "ruin" of America and still opposes public employee unionism. But Ross and I made a connection and crossed the divide, committed to telling the whole story and legacy of eight months in the life of a county.

My message to the guys who were giving me five minutes became very simple: "Ross Sines is giving me hours! If you want your side of the story to be told, I need more time."

They gave it to me.

Any failures in placing the strike and its people in an accurate context are mine.

PICKET LINES ON THE GARRETT COUNTY ROADS

August 4, 1970

On a mild August morning, Don "Toby" Colaw Jr. reported to Oakland's town parking lot ready for a fight. Toby had heard that the county commissioners were planning on shuttling scabs through the picket lines. They planned to launch their secret effort from the parking lot situated between the B&O railroad tracks to the east and the Little Youghiogheny River to the west.

Two of the three Garrett County commissioners had fired Toby's father, Don Colaw Sr., one of 139 workers put out of work and walking the line since April 7. The strikers vowed to hold the line until the anti-union commissioners, Ross Sines and Hubert Friend, recognized American Federation of Municipal Employees (AFSCME) Local 1834. Only Commissioner Allen S. "Dick" Paugh supported recognition. All three commissioners were farmers.

None had ever belonged to a union.

It wasn't the elder Colaw's first time trying to organize a union. After returning home from WWII Navy service in the South Pacific in the 1950s, Colaw joined a United Mineworkers organizing drive at KRAY Coal Co. in Crellin, just outside of Oakland. When the drive failed, the company fired the elder Colaw and evicted him from his company-owned house.

Nobody had known the commissioners' assembly point for the strikebreakers until the prior evening, when Beverly Jean Spiker—wife of road workers' union stalwart Tom Spiker—called Ross Sines.

On the phone call, Mrs. Spiker from the Potomac River coal

mining town of Kitzmiller (17 miles east of Oakland), feigned a Southern belle drawl. She asked Sines where her "husband" could get a job replacing the striking road workers. Within minutes after Sines confirmed the location, union members and their supporters from Oakland to Baltimore began preparing for battle.

Colaw Jr., who grew up outside of Oakland, made the trip back to his hometown from Petersburg, West Virginia, where he worked as a meat cutter in a union-organized market.

Before being hired in Petersburg, young Colaw had followed his father's example, leading an organizing drive at Browning's Foodland, Oakland's largest family-owned supermarket. Colaw said he was placed under surveillance by a union-busting firm hired by the Browning family and threatened with discharge if he "kept talking about the union." With scant support for the union among his fellow workers, he quit. The union helped him get his job in Petersburg.

Colaw Jr. brought shoes and clothes to the picket line for the striking families. And he carried a stick.

"My dad told me to get rid of the stick, due to the state police [positioned nearby]," said Colaw. "My father had just gotten sprayed with pepper spray or tear gas during a sit-in [a strike support action led by strikers' wives] at the courthouse," he said.

Bob Brown, Colaw's business agent, who represented the Retail Clerks International Union, Local 27 in Cresaptown, Maryland, outside of Cumberland, joined him on the parking lot. Colaw and Brown took posts near an aging yellow school bus, parked there by the county commissioners to transport the strikebreakers through picket lines.

Lillian Sines, a resident of Friendsville and a descendant of founding settler John Friend, recalled her husband, Bryan Sines (no relation to Commissioner Sines) applying for work during the strike. Lillian said that Bryan had "worked in timber [logging]." Their family "moved a lot," 14 times in all, to places like Independence and Grafton, West Virginia for work.

Lillian added that Bryan had applied for county roads work 10 years before the strike with no success. "There were no members of the Sines family working on the county roads and you couldn't

2

get hired unless you had family there," she said. Although he wasn't related to Commissioner Sines, her husband applied for work during the strike. She said Ross Sines asked her husband, "Can you shoot a gun?" He warned her husband "a bunch of [union] guys from Baltimore were coming up to Garrett County and they might try to kill road workers who would work during the strike."

The commissioners spent public tax dollars to rent the bus and bust the strike. *The Citizen*, a local newspaper, speculated the license plates on the bus were "borrowed" from a County Roads Department truck. The rusted and worn-out bus, like some of the unsafe equipment in the county garage, quickly became a symbol of the county's contempt for the union and its members.

Ernie Gregg, who subsequently served two 12-year stints as a county commissioner, said, "I remember county road worker Delwood "Dagwood" Freeland with icicles hanging off his arms throwing cinders from the back of a truck. That kind of treatment should have been inconceivable [when equipment could have been purchased to do the job]."

Freddie Van Sickle sat in the bus's driver's seat with some strikebreakers behind him. Van Sickle, a local horse trainer, had enthusiastically agreed to cross the picket line, *after* joining with other scabs to negotiate their rates of pay with the two anti-union commissioners.

Ross Sines, elected commissioner in 1966, stood opposite the bus with 75 supporters, mostly area farmers. The son of Pine Grove Church of the Brethren minister and former Commissioner Jonas Sines, Ross Sines had won office by mounting an ambitious door-to-door campaign in the thinly-settled, 664 square-mile county, Maryland's second largest. He promised to keep taxes low and openly questioned whether county money should be invested in building Garrett Community College, already under consideration. County youth whose parents could afford to send them to college always left the county. Why should the rest of the citizens pay more taxes just to keep some college kids closer to home?

Thirty-eight-years-old, clean-shaven, balding, and not much over five feet, Sines was flanked by his towering, long-bearded

3

neighbor Homer Mellott, a Dunkard Brethren preacher. Mellott was holding a Bible. AFSCME's national magazine, *Public Worker*, reported that Mellott and Sines were "passing out tracts on how to find eternal peace."

Both commissioners had already rejected the county clergy's call for peace.

"You Save Souls, We'll Save the County"

As April ripened, farmers tapped the last maple trees and got their equipment ready to plow their fields. Two weeks after the strike began, a group of ministers from the Mountaintop Ministerial Association urged Sines and his fellow commissioner, Hubert Friend, to sit down with the road workers and reach a compromise. Like Sines, Hubert Friend was the son of a commissioner, Asa "Bill" Friend, who had served from 1903 to 1909. The family was descended from Garrett County's first white settler, John Friend Sr., born in Sweden in 1728.

Narrow-faced, tall, and wiry, 65-year old Hubert Friend raised dairy and Angus cattle and grew potatoes on his farm near Deep Creek Lake on Maryland Route 42, between McHenry and Friendsville. Friend's daughter Vera Dunithan said, "Dad was Republican. He was concerned about saving taxpayers' money. He was really into politics." According to Vera, her father, who had 11 brothers and sisters, was "firm in his beliefs, but very generous" and would "help anyone, rich or poor."

At the end of their meeting, Sines admonished the preachers, "You save souls, we'll run the county."

Rev. Don Matthews, a popular preacher, had grown up with Sines in a slice of the southern county that today comprises Swallow Falls State Park, established in 1923. Matthews, author of *The Journey of a Country Preacher*, said he wasn't surprised by Sines' reply to the ministers.

"Ross was always stubborn from the time we were kids," said Matthews, who once saved Sines' life after Sines' tractor rolled over, pinning his leg.

"Most of the ministers supported me," said Sines. "But they

4

were following Rev. George Tichinel, a coal miner."

George Tichinel went to work mining coal after the sixth grade. His son, Rev. Daryl Tichinel, said his dad got a dollar for a five-ton car, "but sometimes he went days when he got nothing because there was more rock than coal." The once hard-drinking Tichinel joined the United Mineworkers and gave credit to unions for bettering the lot of workers. Daryl said he was sure his dad supported the roads strikers.

Sines' stubbornness hardened with the property destruction and threats that followed the beginning of the strike. The *Baltimore Sun* reported that two explosions had targeted fences surrounding Hubert Friend's 115-acre farm. Friend told the paper he was watching television with his wife in the living room when a blast "shattered a section of the barbed wire fence." He said an unused fuse was found near the explosion. The *Sun* reported that the FBI office in Baltimore was "trying to determine if the bombings violated the Hobbs Act, the federal anti-racketeering law."

David Sines, Ross Sines' nephew, recalled his grandfather–the preacher Jonas Sines–picking up roofing nails that were thrown on the road leading to the Sines' family farm.

"Someone even cut the udder off one of Hubert Friends' dairy cows," said David Sines, who was hired after the strike and became an active union member.

On June 26, the *Washington Post* reported on a series of explosions in the wake of the strike: "Dynamitings Heighten Tension in Garrett County Road Strike." The paper wrote that one blast damaged Sines' driveway, and another wrecked a stone fence on Hubert Friend's farm.

Dynamite blasts also hit two bridges. A span crossing Deep Creek Lake, Maryland's largest lake, sustained minor damage. But the about-to-be-decommissioned Cherry Creek Bridge on State Park Road, leading to Deep Creek State Park, was destroyed.

Sines told The *Post* he checked under the hood of his car, looking for explosives before turning the ignition. The *Post* described the vehicle as a "dusty green Chevrolet, with stickers on the rear bumper saying, 'Stop School Pollution. Stop Sex Education,' and 'America Love it or Leave It.'"

"The county roads look like they had a bout with smallpox,"

5

reported the *Post*. "Motorists do not find it amusing. They have begun calling the commissioners demanding that they take action to get the roads repaired."

Jack Sowers, Local 1834's president, told the *Baltimore Sun* that Sines and Friend weren't the only ones facing threats. He said his wife and some of the strikers also received threats and his wife "packed a pistol for several months."

State Police, investigating the explosions, apprehended Paul Cosner, who'd been working in the county's Sang Run quarry for three years when the strike began. The police took him to a bridge that had been damaged near Cranesville Road.

"The State Police said I blowed stuff up," said Cosner. "They asked if I blew the bridge up and accused me of blowing up the Deep Creek Bridge, too." He said that he told investigators, "I would have done a better job than that."

The news conjured images of gangsters to many readers of the *Post* and its cosmopolitan readership. But Lonnie Artice, the son of striker Ray Artice, said dynamite was plentiful in the county back then, used mostly for removing rocks and clearing stumps from farmland. He said his father had a box of long-degraded dynamite in his garage in Accident, Maryland.

Allen Wilhelm recalled a state policeman showing up at his house during a strike of pulpwood cutters. The cop asked his father, Asa Wilhelm, a road worker from the Grantsville garage, if he had dynamite. His father, a Republican leader in his corner of the county bordering Allegany County, took the cop to a place behind his barn where he had dynamite stored to "open up a ditch," said his son.

The cop told him he needed to investigate. Allen was sure his Dad wasn't involved. Perhaps the police were investigating the wrong infraction. "Dad made moonshine. I packed the sugar and the rye in the hollow."

Smokey Stanton, a former Oakland City Council president, attended training sessions for first responders at the FBI's facility in Quantico, Virginia. He said that as late as the 2000s, the bureau continued to cite the bombing of the bridge over Cherry Creek as an incident of "domestic terrorism."

State Police questioned Ray Artice and his fellow striker Danny

Uphold after they were seen near the site of one of the explosions. They explained that they were cutting timber in the area. Police took no further action after transporting the men to Cumberland, where they passed lie detector tests.

In contrast to the gangster imagery, Ray Artice had drawn the eye of AFSCME's photographer while he was relaxing amidst the conflict. Artice and his co-worker George Vitez are shown pitching horseshoes at the Accident garage behind a line of trucks idled by the strike. Artice, the taller, broader man, with dark, close-cropped hair, is clad in a neat work uniform, a watch on one wrist. Vitez wears no shirt, boasting muscles that could be those of a lightweight boxer. A cigarette hangs from his lips. The brim of his cap is creased back-Gregory Peck pitching against Lee Marvin.

Garrett County Roads Employees' Association

The *Post* asked Sines why he and fellow Commissioner Friend refused to recognize the union, but had recognized the Garrett County Roads Employee's Association, formed in 1956. Sines told the paper, "I won't answer that question because I'm not sure I know what the answer is. It's a legal question." He refused further comment.

Sines dodged the more obvious point. Unlike AFSCME, the Garrett County Roads Employees' Association was what was commonly referred to as a "company" union. The association included supervisory employees and wasn't affiliated with a larger, independent organization from which it could draw support or expertise.

While members of the association had negotiated contracts with the commissioners and even struck for one day around 1965, the group was mostly locked into a posture of subservience to the commissioners. Like other company unions, it was local, weak, and homogeneous.

By contrast, AFSCME had honed its reputation in the 1968 Memphis sanitation workers' strike. The union was militant and multinational. It was accumulating victories across the country. In Maryland, it was working to affiliate with other blue-collar groups just like the Garrett County association.

In September, 1968, a few months after rebellions in the wake of Dr. Martin Luther King's assassination, AFSCME led a strike of sanitation workers in Baltimore, winning union recognition and wage increases. One year later, AFSCME organized highway workers in Harford County, Md., another rural, Republican-led county. Workers struck and were arrested for sitting in the county council chambers. But they held out and won union recognition.

Sines told road workers he had no problem continuing to bargain with the roads' association, whose contract with the county was due to expire in June, 1970. Sines said the "good men" of the association shared nothing in common with the "outside agitators" from Baltimore. He praised the work ethic of John Filsinger, a founder of the group and member of its executive committee.

Born in 1926, Filsinger was one of ten children of German immigrants who settled in the George's Creek mining region of Allegany County in 1902. After briefly working in coal mines, his father, Phillip Filsinger, moved with his wife, Mary, to Garrett County and bought a 100-acre farm on Sand Flat Road. They sold eggs, repaired equipment for other farmers, and made moonshine.

In 1955, the Garrett County Roads Department needed a welder and hired John Filsinger, who'd built a reputation as a good mechanic. He pursued the career, leaving school after eighth grade to help his father on the farm while his brothers served in World War II.

"My father could fix anything," said John Filsinger's son, John "Ed" Filsinger Jr., who started working for the county roads department in 1978. John Jr. said his father built his own boat with a 1935 flathead Ford V-8 engine in the middle and a frame of pipe and sheet metal on the top, painted iridescent green.

"The boat could pull a skier [on Deep Creek Lake] and was a great fishing boat, too," said the younger Filsinger.

Tom Holler, another retired road worker and striker's son, said John Filsinger would make gears "rather than going out and buying them."

While he held Filsinger in high esteem, Sines accused other association members of being ripe for indoctrination. He said road workers were sometimes "picked up" [put to work] by the Welfare Board, on which Sines served. "Anyone who would do a bit of work was put on the roads."

"There were some good people among them," said Sines. "But other people were influenced by outsiders, the union people and 'colored folks' from Baltimore. They didn't think for themselves… just followed union leaders making promises."

While Sines expressed pride in his self-reliance as a farmer, he derided some of the striking road workers who had grown up on family farms and still managed them on the side as followers, not leaders. "They were small farmers who didn't need much education," said Sines. They required foremen "to direct them."

Sines never worked outside of his family farm. Into his 80s, he remained proud that he never accepted Social Security. "My family was never on welfare, and we never took charity. I remember making $278.13 for a year's work. We had a big garden, milk cows and hogs and never went hungry," said Sines, whose farm work earned him a deferment from the draft.

Sines' obstinacy only succeeded in alienating skilled workers like John Filsinger, pushing them to ally with their lesser skilled co-workers. The Commissioner's hard line forged a common cause between white workers from Garrett County and black and white trade unionists from Baltimore, Hagerstown, Cumberland and beyond.

John Filsinger's daughter, Deb Wine Frantz, summed it up: "My daddy was a devout Catholic who was always about being fair. About fair pay. Those boys [road workers] worked hard."

"Unions Don't Belong Here"

Sines' brother, like many Garrett County natives, had traveled to Baltimore to work at well-paying union jobs at Bethlehem Steel. But Sines said, "The unions only belong in the private sector. They don't belong in the public sector. We sent out the tax bills. The bills didn't say if you're dissatisfied, you didn't have to pay. If we couldn't negotiate for the people, the workers had no right to receive their pay."

He added, "The strike wasn't over wages. The union wanted control. But you couldn't run a bunch of men if you couldn't fire anybody."

9

Most of the county's farmers supported Sines. The Garrett County Farm Bureau's newsletter denounced the attacks against property during the strike. The group called for an end to "compulsory unionism in Maryland, prohibiting strikes in certain areas that work against the public interest, and prohibiting violence in labor disputes…"

The farmers, however, had their own history of violent confrontation. In December, 1953, workers at the Imperial Ice Cream processing plant in Oakland went on strike for recognition of District 50 of the United Mineworkers, the union that represented workers at refractory brick plants in nearby Jennings (Garrett County), Mount Savage, and Zihlman (both Allegany County).

The idling of Imperial's plant left 300 dairy farmers from Garrett County and Preston and Tucker Counties in West Virginia with 20,000 gallons of unprocessed milk. *The Republican* newspaper's front page shows a photo of the District 50 organizer's car overturned by farmers. The paper reported that men, "assumed to be farmers," had jumped and injured a striker, Albert Uphole.

The Republican further reported that farmers and strikers held a meeting at the county jail to "settle their difficulties and get the plant working again."

"You Can Eat Groundhogs and Dandelions"

Seventeen years after the Imperial Ice Cream strike, no meetings were held between farmers and union members to get road workers back on the job. Sines said he was convinced the majority of the county residents, like the farmers, supported his refusal to grant union recognition.

Sines also claimed the support of the area's chief business leaders. They included members of the Naylor family that owned hardware and sundry stores. During the Great Depression, they began scooping up mortgages about to foreclose and, by Sines' recollection, acquired about two-thirds of all the mortgages in the county. Even if that's a bit of an exaggeration, it was still enough to fill a roll top desk.

Also fervently opposing unions and goading on Sines was Irvin Feld, the owner of HP (Half-Price) Stores, a company headquartered in the county that was establishing dozens of outlets in the region. Sines' business allies also included the influential Browning supermarket family that had already defeated a union drive by Toby Colaw, the striker's son.

While acknowledging the support of the wealthier members of the community, who controlled the local banks, Sines said he never saw himself as part of the elite. "I could have qualified for food stamps myself," said the farmer from Swallow Falls, who continued to write off the growing union support.

On June 6 and July 16, AFSCME organized caravans of strike supporters, who filled their vehicles with food and clothing in Baltimore and picked up additional vehicles and supplies in Hagerstown and Cumberland, amassing up to 200 cars that rolled into Oakland.

Even Garrett County residents opposed to the union supported the food and clothing efforts. Real estate agent Tom Bernard provided a building for strikers across from a Wal-Mart now on Route 219 to distribute food and clothes.

"Some of the road workers asked if they could use the place," said Bernard. "I'm a Christian. I'm not a union guy or anything like that. But some of the guys were hurting to make it. When people go on strike, not all the people want to strike. Guys who live paycheck-to-paycheck have to go along with it."

Bernard continued, "I told the union members, 'Just use it [the building]. The building was just studding. They put coat hangers on nails. They had a tremendous amount of stuff. I stopped in from time to time."

Despite the help coming from inside and outside the county, by August the four months without paychecks was taking a toll. A man would catch a few trout fly fishing on the Youghiogheny River, but it wasn't enough to keep body and soul alive.

Prior to gathering in the parking lot, leaders on both sides sent out dire warnings of bloodshed if the strike was not settled. Not only had the commissioners fired the strikers, but they also sought court injunctions to limit their pickets and the caravans of union supporters from the east. The commissioners were continuing to pay 13 roads department workers who had refused to strike but had performed no work since April 7.

The would-be strikebreakers included Owen Bach, a founder of the roads employees' association, a resident of Accident, Md. and a veteran of World War II. Mary Bach, his widow, said Owen had nearly lost his leg during the Battle of the Bulge. Medics saw his hand sticking out of the sand, dug him out and administered penicillin. He spent nine months in the hospital. When he came back home, she said, "He took a long time to get himself right [emotionally]."

Owen Bach worked closely with Leo Rinker, a road worker and neighbor, who was wounded on the Belgian front during the war. Mary Bach remembers packing lunch buckets for both men. Leo was a strike leader, and later a president of AFSCME Local 1834. But Owen refused to strike and never joined the union.

"Owen told me, 'I almost gave my life to my country, and I don't want to live in turmoil with someone [a union] telling me what to do,'" said Mary Bach. "Owen felt God had been good to him. He had good wages and benefits and didn't need a union."

Bach's co-workers, their wives and families didn't share his satisfaction with wages and benefits. Lonnie Artice, son of striker Ray Artice, and Tom Holler, son of striker Lyden Holler, both remember "Hard Time Sines," the self-described poor dirt farmer, telling strikers' families they could "eat groundhogs and dandelions" if their fathers and husbands didn't want to return to work.

Tom Holler said Sines told his constituents he was saving the county money by keeping payroll costs low on the county roads. "But it wasn't *his* money. It was the *taxpayers'* money, and I always thought my father and I worked *for* the taxpayers," said Holler, who frequently walked the picket line with his father during the strike.

"There Will Be Bloodshed"

On July 23, as the hay lay bailed in the fields, Commissioner Allen S. Paugh Sr. wrote to Maryland Governor Marvin Mandel asking for mediation of the conflict.

Sixty-three years old, broad-shouldered, with gentle but intense eyes, Paugh sported a crew cut and looked like a football coach. He'd won a reputation across partisan lines as a reasonable and effective commissioner since his election in 1962.

"Dick Paugh was a humble, soft-spoken man," said Lowell Bender, who worked closely with Paugh on the board of the Garrett County Community Action Committee (GCCAC) and as a supporter of Garrett County Community College.

"No one worked harder than my father," said his son, Carroll Paugh, a county school bus owner-operator. Growing up in a farmhouse built in 1914, with 16 brothers and sisters, his father, he said, "Never learned to play."

While Paugh waited on an answer to his request for mediation, *The Citizen*, published by Finzel, Maryland resident and county surveyor Virginia Rosenbaum, proposed a taxpayer protest because roads were not being repaired.

Curtis Nazelrod, son of striker Eugene Otis Nazelrod, a twice-wounded World War II veteran, said his father had done some roadwork for Rosenbaum while working on nearby county roads. Eugene Nazelrod, his son, asked Rosenbaum to cover the strike with an "unbiased opinion," unlike *The Republican* and the Cumberland newspaper that, he said, mostly opposed the union.

Rosenbaum consistently criticized the anti-union commissioners over the course of the conflict. In an editorial she wrote: "Commissioners have been told by two policing bodies [State Police and Garrett County Sheriff's office] that they "cannot wet-nurse men trying to take other men's jobs and that only limited protection could be given [to strikebreakers]."

"If the commissioners persisted in trying to 'get men across the picket line,'" *The Citizen* speculated, "there will be bloodshed, make no bones about that! This has been a peaceful strike so far, but the old-time Union leaders are beginning to say, 'See we told you so.' This peaceful method produced nothing."

Rosenbaum never wavered in challenging the commissioners during and after the strike.

"I have a hole in my chest from Virginia Rosenbaum's finger," said subsequent Garrett County Commissioner Ernie Gregg, a local

13

pharmacist who drew the libertarian publisher's ire in the years following the strike for supporting the fluoridation of drinking water.

On July 29, an article in the *Baltimore Sun* quoted Wellington "Jack" Sowers, AFSCME Local 1834's president: "Yup, we're all a bunch of mean hillbillies." Described by The *Sun* as "the wiry, tobacco-chewing president of the county road workers' new union," Sowers continued, "Hell, we're not violent people, but we're going to draw some blood if the commissioners try to send some men out to work on those roads."

Another striker, Cecil Welch, 45, described as a "fired [county roads] truck driver," told the *Sun,* "By God, there's one thing about it — I'll fight for my job." *The Sun* said Welch's vow drew a "Yes sir," from Salem Shreve, 51, an Oakland "native and [county roads] laborer for the past 15 years."

The Sun reported that, in preparation for bringing in strikebreakers, the county's National Guard Armory in Oakland was prepared to have "precautionary contingents" of state policemen.

The Sun described Commissioner Paugh as a "burly farmer who has been cast in the role of the county's maverick commissioner." Paugh told the paper: "There's going to be bloodshed if those two [Sines and Friend] try to break this strike. [They] won't tell me what they're going to do. But I've been a working man all my life and I'll fight for the working man. I can't blame the men a bit for holding out. I'd fight for my job, too."

The Republican reported: "Mr. Paugh said yesterday that some 95 percent of the county's school children travel to consolidated schools by bus on the 739 miles of roads which need repair." The paper added: "Eighty-six school bus drivers, independent contractors, were prepared to refuse to drive because of the poor condition of the roads." Paugh added that the county was in "excellent state financially and is financially able to give the road workers a raise."

No Mediation

On July 27, Governor Mandel told Commissioner Paugh that Sines and Friend had rebuffed the mediation request. Confrontation appeared to be inevitable. Three days later, *The Republican* reported that

Edmond Grovner, Mandel's chief administrative assistant, reiterated that the governor would not intervene in the dispute "unless he was guaranteed cooperation on both sides."

Hubert Friend, the county commission's president, announced the county was ready to put 100 strikebreakers on the job with police escort.

In a July 30 editorial, *The Citizen* attacked Friend and Sines for continuing to collect taxes to pay non-striking roads employees idled by the strike. The editor again offered to help organize a taxpayer's revolt.

The *Baltimore Sun* reported that Sines and Friend asked Mandel to call out the National Guard to protect replacement workers but were told the military would only be called in an "emergency, while newly hired road workers were refusing to begin work until their safety was assured.

On August 3, The *Sun* reported Sines and Friend had rejected a last-minute plan by Joseph J. Biondo, a federal mediator from Pittsburgh, to settle the strike after a two-hour closed-door meeting with Circuit Court Judge Stuart F. Hamill and lawyers representing both the county commissioners and AFSCME.

"The rejected [union] plan," reported *The Sun*, "would have provided for the striking road workers to return to work immediately and take a further vote on their union affiliation after Election Day in November."

The paper again echoed the union leaders' prediction of violence if the commissioners tried to put replacement workers on the job.

"Nobody is Going to Take Our Members' Jobs"

Ray Metz organized and served as president of the union's first State Highway Department local in Maryland, located in nearby LaVale, outside of Cumberland. He had traveled to Garrett County and helped organize the road workers, winning an appointment to AFSCME's staff after the strike.

Metz recalled that on August 4, Andy Lewis, secretary treasurer of the Maryland AFL-CIO, called Gov. Mandel from the AFSCME office in Cumberland.

"The conversation with the governor was very frank," said Metz. Secretary Treasurer Lewis told Mandel, "We are meeting those scabs in Oakland tomorrow in force. We don't want any bloodshed. But nobody is going to take our members' jobs."

Sines also called the governor. "I yelled and said if there's any bloodshed, it's on his hands." Sines blamed the governor for failing to arrest strikers who were breaking the law.

Captain William E. O'Hara, commander of the Maryland State Police in Western Maryland, assisted by Lieutenant Sam Conrad from LaVale, positioned 40 state troopers at the scene, alongside Garrett County Sheriff Frantz and his deputy, Frank Finch.

Frank Finch's precarious position reflected the complexity of the strike in the tight-knit county. His father, Bill Finch, was an outspoken roads striker. His mother, Kathleen Finch, was unwavering in her support of her husband and his union. Kathleen Finch told AFSCME's newspaper: "Bill was worried Frank would get hurt [during the bus battle], and Frank was worried his daddy would get arrested."

Four months of pent-up anger over the road workers' firings could not be contained forever. Families were hurting. Bellies were aching. The barren fields of winter would soon be upon them.

THE BATTLE ON THE BUS

Busting Up the Bus

On that fateful August morning, union members from Baltimore and Garrett County carrying clubs faced the yellow school bus where would-be strike breakers were preparing to cross the picket line. Freddie Van Sickle sat in the driver's seat waiting for the signal to fire up the old diesel engine. A grim-faced Commissioner Sines stood beside the bus with 65 supporters standing with him.

The union men surged forward. They forced Van Sickle and the strikebreakers from the school bus. They busted the windshield, jerked out the ignition wires and flattened the tires.

"I remember big boards with spikes driven through them being put under the tires," said Helen Fike, wife of striker Jim Fike, who had joined a sit-in with other wives at the courthouse at the start of the strike. The wives had blocked Hubert Friend from leaving his office at the end of the workday, forcing him to call the deputy sheriffs for safe passage.

Toby Colaw joined the union members storming the bus. He said one of the union's leaders from Cumberland asked if he knew where a can of gasoline could be found to torch the bus.

Victor Nazelrod Jr., son of a striker, said one of the strikebreakers sprayed ether [a component of tear gas] at the union members taking over the bus. The younger Nazelrod had been living in Silver Spring, Maryland where he completed a government-sponsored machinist apprenticeship, making gun and tank parts.

"I used to come back and walk the picket lines with my dad," said Nazelrod, who remembered attending rallies on the courthouse lawn. He later went to work for the State Highway Department in Garrett County, joining AFSCME.

Strikers and leaders of AFSCME Council 67 in Baltimore took over the bus. Photos show excited, intensely serious men ready to challenge any authorities who might try to remove them.

After the strikers took over the bus, State Police warned a union representative from Baltimore who was addressing strikebreakers to stop "agitating" the crowd. They said the same to Martha Glotfelty, a union opponent and administrative secretary at the roads department supporting Sines and Friend.

No arrests were made for destroying the bus. But two residents were arrested nearby. Tom Skipper, a newly hired strikebreaker from Swallows Falls, was apprehended for carrying a 22-caliber unloaded revolver. Skipper said he was threatened with "bodily harm before he tried to go to work" and was later released without charge.

Friendsville resident Harry Faucett was charged with assaulting Jack Eisenberg, a freelance photographer hired by AFSCME who had been "having words" with some of the farmers supporting Sines and Friend. Eisenberg swore out a warrant. Faucett was charged with assault and posted $23.75 in bail.

James R. Spear, a State Highway Department worker from Friendsville who grew up with Faucett said, "I don't know why Harry [Faucett] opposed the strike." Faucett later went to work for the railroad and was a member of one of the railroad unions. There, Faucett earned a living wage, said Spear, who helped sign up his co-workers as AFSCME members. Spear later served for 20 years on the Friendsville City Council and was elected mayor in the late 1990's.

"I have to commend the law enforcement officers for their restraint," said Ray Metz. "They only stepped in when someone could be hurt. They came in with orders from the governor [Mandel] to act that way."

"Cops Didn't Do Their Jobs!"

Directly following the confrontation, State Police escorted Sines, Friend and the newly hired road workers to a meeting in the Masonic

Order's auditorium inside Oakland's National Bank building. Garrett County State's Attorney Fred Thayer and Cumberland attorney Miller Bowen accompanied the commissioners, temporarily replacing vacationing Garrett County Attorney W. Dwight Stover.

Although the meeting was closed to the press, *The Citizen* reported that participants could be heard "when they got loud."

Several persons, including Martha Glotfelty, reportedly "were accusing the State Police of not doing their jobs." The police answered that the strike was a civil matter, but pledged to "follow up any warrants" sworn out by citizens against the men who damaged the bus and arrest the accused.

David Ettlin, a cub reporter for the *Baltimore Sun* at the beginning of his four-decade newspaper career, followed the county delegation and workers to the meeting. Gathered outside the auditorium with other reporters, his ear against the door, Ettlin heard someone loudly excoriating the police for not making any arrests in the vandalizing of the bus. He said he heard someone say, "We don't have any 'Ni--ers' in this county – why did you let those 'N--ers' on the bus?"

Years later, Sines said he didn't remember the meeting. But, when asked why the strike lasted for more than seven months, he blamed [Blacks] from Baltimore's AFSCME Council 67 for prolonging the conflict.

In a September 9, 1970 article in *The Sun* headlined "Garrett County Insulated to Change from Outsiders," Thomas B. Edsall wrote that Sines repeated the same assertion to another reporter.

During the strike, *The Republican* printed several letters attacking the union from former Garrett County State Senator Clifford Friend. In an August 13 letter that invoked racist images, Friend asked if the lack of arrests during the battle of the bus meant that "union hirelings from elsewhere can feel free to come up here and commit rape against our property and people without being punished."

All Work Stopped

After the meeting at the bank, union advocates and opponents remained on or near the parking lot for several hours, dispersing only after Bowen, the temporary county attorney, announced that no newly hired road workers would be put on the job.

In a press statement, Sines and Friend said it was "futile" to try to employ new workers because of the "opposition of a number of former roads employees and the mob from other areas in the state and possibly from out of state…We do not want a catastrophe or violence."

Victor Nazelrod Jr., said he believed the food, clothing and financial support his father and other workers received from union members in Baltimore were decisive in avoiding a violent confrontation.

"If it wasn't for that support," he said, "there's no telling what might have happened." Victor Nazelrod's cousin, Curtis Nazelrod, said, "I heard Ross Sines said his life was in danger. Let me tell you, if the strikers had wanted to 'take out' Ross Sines, they would have."

The Race Card

AFSCME staffers weren't surprised by the loud, racist language from behind the door of the Masonic Order's auditorium. To the union's organizers, Black men showing up in a white Appalachian town were just doing their job, like the white union supporters who had arrived in the Black community of Memphis two years prior to support the city sanitation workers. America was and is racially divided. But AFSCME leaders and organizers called for white and Black workers to stand on the same side to win as the caravans arrived.

"Sixty-two automobiles were in [a] parade, including several carloads of Black AFSCME members from Baltimore," wrote Rosenbaum. "Raymond Clark, the Black president of the Baltimore local, spoke and was applauded on several occasions by the workers. This is the first time many Garrett County people were exposed to their Black brothers, as there are very few, if any, Negroes in Garrett County."

Starting out by acknowledging racism in the wider society, Rosenbaum then played her own race card, seeking to turn the county's racial bias against the commissioners instead of the union.

20

"The appearance of the Negroes had a dampening effect on trade in Oakland, however as the streets were reported to be almost devoid of shoppers…In all probability, there will be more of this show of Black strength since no one knows better than the Blacks what it is to feel the oppression of authority that dogmatically refuses to talk."

She continued, "… it has been reported to this newspaper that Blacks found Deep Creek Lake very attractive as a summer resort. The County Commissioners will be pleased to learn that they have opened up a new avenue of vacation money for Garrett County since, by their refusal to talk with representatives of AFSCME, the Baltimore people saw the beautiful Garrett County vacation sites for the first time."

Some strikers and their families, looking for a way to win and get back to work, saw the Black union members from Baltimore as critical to settling the strike. "One thing that helped us a lot," said striker Sheldon Whitacre, was "a lot of Black people coming in [to support the strike]. It scared them [Sines and Friend] to death."

Oakland Attorney Tom Doyle, an avowedly right-wing Republican, rejected Whitacre's assessment, saying he didn't think race "played a major role" in how residents viewed AFSCME or the strike. Doyle did, however, recall the prevalence of "revert-back" clauses in land instruments in Garrett County that prevented the sale of properties—including former church buildings—to Blacks.

While union officials and the commissioners contended over the strike's legality, citizens were more concerned about the deterioration of the roads. Many taxpayers showed up at commission meetings complaining about potholes. They included county resident Michael Phillippi, who, on Aug. 31, presented the commission with a bill for automobile repairs he said were caused by poorly maintained roads. The commission declined.

Dave Ramsey carried an indelible memory of the failing roads. Ramsey, who worked for the Garrett County Community Action Committee (GCCAC), hit a pothole while driving with his pregnant wife, Sara, a teacher at Southern High School. The jolt triggered Sara's contractions. "My daughter was born after we hit that pothole," he said.

Battle Renewed

Federal mediator Joseph Biondo repeated his offer to help resolve the dispute, but Sines and the union leadership pledged to continue their battle, with both sides hoping the parking lot confrontation would expand support for their side.

The Republican reported: "Sines wouldn't divulge additional plans" but said he hoped "there would be a great swelling of those sympathizing with the new workers [replacement workers] who would far outnumber the union sympathizers." The newly-hired road workers were told to continue to report to work each day.

AFSCME leader Ernest B. "Ernie" Crofoot (1924-2013), one of the union's staffers recruited from the shop floor of southeast Baltimore County's Glenn L. Martin aviation plant, vowed the union would return in force if the commissioners once again tried to break the strike.

The Citizen listed the names of newly hired employees and their supporters who were in the parking lot on August 4, advising that, if names were wrong, they could be "corrected" in the next issue.

The list included: Dell Rumms, Sam Thomas, Webster Brenneman, Leo Spiker, Lee Moats, Clifford Frantz, Joseph Friend, Larry Lewis, Tom Skipper, Carl Savage, Paul Mellott, William Brenneman, Kenith Buckle, Roy Broadwater, Elbert Buckle, Owen Stanton, Herbert Buckle, George Shawley, James Glotfelty, Hobert Buckle, Alvin Brenneman, David Hinebaugh, Fred VanSickle, Pose Dewitt, Roger Bond, Robert Enlow, Adrian Spiker, Paul Hoye, Ben Savage, George Bishoff, Nelson Alexander, Robert Detrick, Marlin Thomas, Marvin Thomas, Rusty Thomas, Marvin Sines, Marlen Sines, Hugh Reams, Ervin Lowdermilk, Joe Dewitt, Claude Fike, Owen Bach, Paul Frazee, Bid Moles, Parley Savage, Waldo Zinken, Jake Jones, Ray Doerr, Bill Umble, Ronnie Durr, Clark Schlosnagle, Eddie Groves, Harry Faucett and Mrs. Martha Glotfelty.

The Republican: "Naked Power Exhibited"

Summing up the tense day in the parking lot, *The Republican*'s editorial read: "…Naked power was exhibited in Oakland and it wasn't a pretty picture…This has nothing to do with the value of unionism and the right of workers to organize if that is their desire."

The paper continued, "Is law by force to be the pattern of the future? 'You do what we want or else?' Just naked power by force of numbers? Is this what we are going to be forced to live with? When law and order break down we are headed for anarchy. Are we on that road?"

The newspaper echoed Sines' criticism of the State Police: "There were forty State Police in the area and also county authorities. They made no attempt to prevent the bus from being boarded illegally. They prevented a riot, yes, but what did they do to preserve court orders?"

The Republican alleged that store owners were also threatened: "Merchants have been pressured into contributing to the support of the strikers, for fear of retaliation and boycott."

Elections

Twenty-one candidates had put their names in nomination for the September 15 primary for county commissioner. If the strike wasn't settled, the conflict would be the central focus of the general election. For AFSCME Local 1834 to win the strike, the county would need to elect new commissioners who would recognize the union.

One day after the battle of the bus, Governor Mandel and U.S. Senator Joseph Tydings campaigned for re-election in Garrett County. The *Baltimore Sun* reported that Mandel gave a ten-minute speech at Wisp Resort. He was introduced by William Goldsborough, a leading Garrett County Democrat. Goldsborough was a member of the state roads commission, later appointed by Mandel to the state's board of education. According to reports, Mandel didn't mention the roads strike.

But Senator Tydings couldn't ignore the conflict. A resident of Harford County, he had been elected to the U.S. Senate in 1964, defeating J. Glenn Beall Sr., a native of Cumberland. Tydings was facing a stiff primary election fight with George P. Mahoney, who was attacking him for sponsorship of gun registration, Tydings visited the county road workers on their picket line at the Accident garage to talk about both the strike and gun control.

The Citizen's August 6th issue published a photo of Tydings addressing strikers in Accident.

"When working men get together and want to have a union," he said, "they should have that right. It is my understanding that the county recognized the Association, so long as it's called an Association, and when it became affiliated and called itself a union, it was not recognized and it does not seem to me to be fair. Insofar as this specific is concerned, I think the federal mediator's recommendations should be considered."

The Republican reported that before the governor and senator left town, Commissioner Dick Paugh gave Mandel a painting of a Garrett County farmhouse, produced by county resident Harland Bittinger.

The strike had whipped up unprecedented interest in Garrett County's September primary election, with 52 percent of registered voters turning out, among the highest in the nation that year.

Deadlock

Three weeks after the battle of the bus, Paul Cosner pleaded guilty to "willful and malicious destruction" of the fence surrounding Commissioner Friends' farm on June 16. Circuit Court Judge Stuart Hamill revoked Cosner's $200 bond and ordered him to the county jail for a one year sentence.

"First I was locked up in Baltimore," said Cosner in a 2019 interview. "Then I was sent to Patuxent Institution [for the criminally insane]. They said I was mentally damaged." Cosner served the rest of his time in the state prison in Hagerstown.

While bloodshed had been averted, tensions were still high. Hubert Friend, Sines' gentle Methodist partner, could have brought the strike to a close months before. Years later, many residents said the firings and the strike might never have happened if the brash, younger Sines had not pushed Friend into the morass.

But four months had passed – more than 20 weeks of working men left to make their way without paychecks and spouses determined to stand by their husbands and their right to form a union. Interviewed in 2020, Sines explained how four months of escalating rancor had hardened Friend's will and his contempt for the strikers.

Defending his characterization of strikers as mobsters, Sines said that Martha Glotfelty, the anti-union secretary of the roads department, "almost had her clothes torn off her [by strikers' wives]." He added, "Some of the strikers approached Hubert Friend and told him, "Your face could wear out three bodies. What kind of people treat a man like that?"

Thousands of county residents were asking "what kind of people" would fire a whole department of county employees, tell them to live on "groundhogs and dandelions" and leave roads and bridges to deteriorate, all to keep from recognizing a union?

3

IT ALL BEGAN A LONG TIME AGO

Maryland's Wilderness County 1750-1950

"The railroad, the Baltimore and Ohio, introduced a new aspect of western civilization to Glade Country highlanders of nineteenth century western Maryland—industrialism. Industrialists of the late nineteenth century came to the Maryland mountains in pursuit of the dollars generated by capitalists and industrialists in pursuit of summertime fun. Garrett County came of age by the twentieth century as a coal county, a timber county, a resort county, an agricultural county." [1]

Located 176 miles west of Baltimore, Garrett County borders Pennsylvania and West Virginia, accessible by Interstate Route 68, completed in 1993. Named for John W. Garrett, the former president of the B&O Railroad, the county's 656 square miles make it Maryland's second largest.

Once part of Frederick County, then Allegany County until 1872, Garrett County spans the Continental Divide of the Appalachian Mountains. Its western slopes drain into the Youghiogheny River ("the Yough"), then the Ohio, then the Mississippi, then the Gulf. The eastern slope flows into the Savage River, which empties into the Potomac, the Chesapeake Bay and the Atlantic Ocean. Forests cover seven out of every 10 acres of land in Garrett County. Seventy thousand acres are in state-owned parcels. [2]

Indigenous Americans hunted and fished in the Garrett County region for four thousand years prior to the arrival of white settlers. The Youghiogheny, Massawomecks, Delawares, Senecas and Iroquois were said to inhabit or visit parts of the current county, favoring the area's rivers. [3]

The Youghiogheny River Band of Shawnees, led by Chief Joseph "Raincrow" Neal was reconstituted in the 1980s. In 1994, the band was granted land around Friendsville, Md. by Jim "Pappy" Ross Sr., who claimed ancestry from both John Friend and the Shawnee. The history of indigenous Americans in Garrett County is a subject of ongoing study, aided by the preservation of 49,000 artifacts unearthed by archeologists during the building of I-68 In 1972.

White men first came to present-day Garrett County in 1750 searching for a passage to the West.

In 1754, George Washington was barracked at Fort Necessity, just 57 miles west of Garrett County's seat of Oakland. Washington surrendered to the French, marking the start of the French and Indian Wars (1753 to 1763). By 1763, only a single village of indigenous Americans inhabited the banks of the "Yough," the others driven west by the war.

The first permanent white resident of present-day Garrett County was Swedish-born John Friend, who arrived in 1763. By 1776, there were around a dozen settler families in the area.

Battles of the American Revolution never extended onto the current county's terrain, although major battles were fought in nearby Virginia, in the region that became West Virginia in 1863.

In 1780, indigenous tribes allied with the British engaged in military action against settlers around the Cheat River, 46 miles west of Oakland in what is now West Virginia.

After the war, the new federal government sought to encourage settlement in the Maryland hills. The government allotted more than 2,500 fifty-acre lots in Western Maryland for settlement by Revolutionary War veterans. [4]

Bear hunter Meshach Browning, born in 1781, is the earliest folk hero of the wilderness county. His memoir, *Forty-Four Years of the Life of a Hunter*, is still popular.

In 1789, the Maryland General Assembly authorized the establishment of Allegany County, including the area that is now Garrett County. The 1790 federal census of Allegany County listed 4,800 people, 258 of whom were Black slaves.

In 1794, President Washington returned to Western Maryland

27

and appeared in military uniform at Fort Cumberland, where he dispatched troops to stanch the Whiskey Rebellion, launched by farmers who were refusing to pay an excise tax on the whiskey they sold.

In 1842, the B&O Railroad was cut through to Allegany County, opening the Port of Baltimore to coal and timber from the west.

White Europeans and Black Slaves

The mid-1800's saw a spike in immigration, as Germans, many of them Amish and Mennonite, settled in today's Garrett County, voyaging from their home nation or from nearby Pennsylvania.

Slavery was an important part of the local economy in Allegany County. In her book, *Everyone Counts. A history of African American enslavement in Allegany County, Maryland*, Allegany College of Maryland historian Lynn Bowman writes: "[The enslaved] … slipped through the cracks of history here, perhaps largely because they represented an inconvenient and embarrassing truth: that the initial success of Allegany County was dependent upon slavery."

By 1830, one out of every 13 residents in Allegany County was enslaved. Bowman described the "peculiarities of slavery in Allegany County, which are unique even from its neighboring counties to the north and the south."

The hilly, rocky terrain, she wrote, was not suitable for large-scale plantations. As a result, slaves in the region were primarily used to build roads and buildings and to labor at taverns—roadside hotels that attended to the needs of visitors, maintaining their carts, carriages and harnesses etc. [5]

A chapter of Bowman's book describes the tavern-operating Tomlinson family in Grantsville, whose descendant Jesse Tomlinson owned slaves and served in the Maryland legislature. Tomlinson granted freedom to his slaves one year before his death in 1839.

Western Maryland was border territory during the Civil War. A total of 728 residents, free and slave, of present-day Garrett County fought in the conflict, most of them for the Union. [6]

Several prominent Garrett County residents enslaved Black people. James Drane, builder of the longest-standing settler house in the county, owned six slaves, and U.S. Secretary of War James McHenry owned ten slaves. [7]

In 1859, John W. Garrett transported the first military troops aboard a U.S. railroad to crush John Brown's raid on Harper's Ferry. A few weeks later, he paraded through the streets of Baltimore alongside Army Colonel Robert E. Lee.

But Garrett put his business interests first, choosing to become an ally and confidante of President Abraham Lincoln. The Pennsylvania Railroad and other B&O competitors sought to profit from increased western shipments, while the railroad endured repeated Confederate assaults on its infrastructure, including bridges. [8]

Garrett intensified his aid to Lincoln and the Union Army. He built fortified cars to carry troops, played a decisive role in protecting Washington, D.C. and was instrumental in keeping Maryland out of the Confederacy. The B&O was labeled "Mr. Lincoln's Railroad." Lincoln demonstrated his appreciation by appointing Edwin D. Stanton, a former attorney for the Garrett family's business enterprises, secretary of Defense.

The city of Oakland, founded in 1823 by Isaac McCarty, a slave owner, was twice invaded by the rebel army and defended by Union troops. Stations on the Underground Railroad were tucked into the terrain, with armed posses seeking to capture runaway slaves.

Emmanuel Episcopal Church in Cumberland, built on the site of the former Fort Cumberland, opened the tunnels under the old fort to escaping enslaved people. Stephen Willis Friend of Sang Run (today's Garrett County) operated a stop on the Underground Railroad, running afoul of his slave-owning neighbors from the Hoye family when one of their enslaved joined a slave that Friend was harboring. [9]

The 1900 census listed 128 people of color in Garrett County (119 Black, 9 Mixed Race). [10] Black residents in Mountain Lake Park, outside of Oakland, included well-known entrepreneurs such as Richard Moore Sr., a barber, who worked in hotels in Mountain Lake Park and Loch Lynn between 1890 and 1920. Jack McGuffin, a Black landowner and wagon driver, and his wife, Martha, a laundress, lived in Mountain Lake Park in the early 1900s. Before they both died in the early 1930s in Loch Lynn, Jack McGuffin had gone to work in the pea cannery located in that town.

Racial discrimination in employment was widespread. An 1899 want ad in *The Republican* for Hotel Chautauqua solicited white women only for positions as "waiter girls" and chambermaids. Black and white women were asked to apply as laundry women. [11]

By 1930, Jack and Martha McGuffin were the only Black persons listed in the census for district seven, comprising Mountain Lake Park and Loch Lynn. [12]

Note: The history and influence of Black people in Garrett County is the subject of ongoing research. In 2021, Mayor Don Sincell of Mountain Lake Park, in conjunction with the county's NAACP chapter and the Mountain Lake Park Historical Association, acquired grant funding to move Bethel A.M.E. Church, a historic Black place of worship from Pleasant Valley, where it had been used as a blacksmith shop, to Mountain Lake Park. Plans for Bethel Center include additional research into the roots of Garrett County's Black community research and the cultural, political, and economic factors that led to the exodus of most Black families from Garrett County by the 1930s. Research has also uncovered the graves of Black Civil War veterans in Oakland's cemetery, where ceremonies commemorating their service have been held.

A Republican County

A frontier philosophy endured. In *Maryland Lost and Found*, Eugene L. Meyer wrote: "In a sense Garrett is to Maryland what Alaska is to the lower forty-eight states, a last frontier far from the population and political centers. It is a place peopled by individualists where resentment of outside government runs deep and rules and regulations are tolerated but seldom welcomed. [13]

The booms and busts of the extraction industries (coal, timber, natural gas) and tourism have only bolstered the residents' self-reliance and wariness of outside political dominance."

All four sectors of the economy rapidly expanded after the

B&O Railroad cut through to Oakland in 1851 and Wheeling, West Virginia a year later. Timber capitalists arrived and opened sawmills, lending their names to towns like Jennings and Crellin. The B&O commissioned The Glades Hotel, inviting elite vacationers from Washington and Baltimore to enjoy the cool weather and mountain streams.

In 1868, John W. Garrett built the Garrett Memorial Stone Church at the corner of Liberty and Second Streets in Oakland. Presidents William Henry Harrison and Grover Cleveland prayed there during visits to hotels erected close by the B&O's western right of way.

Garrett County was officially established in 1872, its residents — most of them of German, Irish and English descent — approving autonomy by a vote of 1297 to 40.

E.S. Zevely, editor of the county newspaper *The Glades Star* (founded 1871), persuasively advocated for autonomy, accusing Allegany leaders in the county's seat in Cumberland of hoarding revenues from their neighbors in what became Garrett County.

Republican advocates of Garrett County promoted separation from Allegany as a wise retort to the recent formation of Wicomico County on Maryland's Democratic Party-dominated Eastern Shore.

Residents considered the name Glades County, but pronounced John W. Garrett the county's namesake, based in part on Garrett's promise to widen his investment there.

Farmers and Workers Organize

In 1875, Garrett County residents organized the county's first fraternal meeting place for farmers — Grange, Cherry Creek No. 144. The hall was one of 12,000 U.S. lodges of the National Grange of the Patrons of Husbandry. The Grange (early term for granary or barn) was an organization of small farmers, not a union. But for a time the group emulated the radicalism of wage laborers in advocating for decent prices for crops, affordable freight rates and mortgages.

Other lodges were formed in McHenry and Oakland in 1876. The Grange's cooperative efforts among farmers in buying equipment and marketing crops hit some rough spots in Maryland, with some

31

members declaring bankruptcy. But the Grange returned by the turn of the century, with thirteen new lodges organized in Garrett County in 1904 and eleven more in 1905, mostly as places to socialize.

In 1877, with the B&O still beset by the Panic of 1873, John W. Garrett imposed a 10-percent wage cut on railroad workers while simultaneously granting a 10-percent increase in the company's dividends.

B&O workers struck, along with workers on the competing Pennsylvania Railroad, initiating the nation's first large-scale general strike. Thousands of railroad workers, coal miners and industrial workers in all the nation's major cities joined the strike.

Garrett convinced President Rutherford B. Hayes to dispatch federal troops to Cumberland to crush strikers on the railroad and in the mines. The wily business man charged the federal government for use of the B&O to transport the troops he had requested.

Garrett and his railroad played a decisive role in defeating chattel slavery. But today, John Work Garrett, who died in Deer Park, Maryland in 1884, is just as prominently remembered as an enforcer of what the railroad unions of his time called "wage slavery." He endures as one of the nation's most infamous union busters.

Coverage in Garrett County's newspaper, *The Republican,* founded in 1877 (the same year as the railroad strike), foreshadowed that newspaper's treatment of class conflicts a century later.

The newspaper acknowledged that "public sympathy" was with the "impoverished" strikers, who faced severely reduced hours and were forced to pay for use of the B&O to and from their work sites.

The paper never mentioned Garrett by name, writing: "We find no reason for charging the Company with a disposition to oppress the employees."

The paper said the reduced days per week were the result of economic conditions, crediting the B&O with an "honorable effort" to give railroad firemen a "chance to make three or four trips a week than to discharge them entirely,"

The Republican defended the 10-percent dividends issued to shareholders, writing: "The firemen are not competent to pass judgment [on the increases] … The ten percent dividend was not deducted from the pay of the Brethren."

Finally, the paper recognized the right of workers to strike but denounced the "threats of violence" as workers went "shop to shop compelling men to quit work." Those roving strikers, wrote *The Republican*, were "becoming common rioters and ought to be treated as such."

In her book, *John W. Garrett and the Baltimore and Ohio Railroad* (Johns Hopkins University Press, 2017), Kathleen Waters Sander wrote: "[Garrett managed] in an authoritarian manner that brought no insubordination from below or second guessing from above. Garrett asserted his dominant and autocratic management style from the start. He quickly gained a reputation as a 'severe economist' and a 'rigid disciplinarian.'"

One year after the Great Railroad Strike, *The Republican* faced competition with the first issue of *Mountain Democrat*, founded in Oakland. The newspaper featured sensational headlines and unabashedly promoted white supremacy.

A 1,300-word letter in a 1901 edition criticized Republican President Theodore Roosevelt's White House dinner with Black leader Booker T. Washington. The writer asked, "If the President of the United States, with all his wealth and his aristocratic antecedents, is willing to have his family sit at dinner with a negro, how is the poor white man in the South to maintain his position of social superiority to the negro?"

❈ ❈ ❈

In 1888, William Luke, who had migrated from Scotland in 1852, founded the Piedmont Pulp and Paper Company, located in Luke in the Potomac River basin at the foot of Backbone Mountain in Allegany County.

In 1919, workers waged a militant but failed strike to organize the paper mill. The powerful paternalism of the Luke family staved off organizing until the CIO finally succeeded in 1946. [14] The mill, bordering the Garrett County town of Bloomington, later operated as Westvaco Pulp and Paper, still under Luke family management. In the 2000s, it was purchased by NewPage, then Verso, employing large numbers of Garrett County residents.

Workers in the paper mill were first represented by members of the United Paperworkers and, many decades later, the United Steelworkers. The first commercially successful sulfite pulp mill in the U.S. required a steady supply of logs. Garrett County residents cut pulpwood to supply the mill.

The area's coal mines were part of the Appalachian Coal field, stretching from Pennsylvania to Alabama. Semi-bituminous coal in Western Maryland was created under more pressure and heat than bituminous (soft) coal, but less than the anthracite (hard coal) found in Northeastern Pennsylvania. It was high in carbon, low in sulfur and highly suitable for producing steam energy.

The first commercial coal mine in Western Maryland was opened in 1792. But large-scale mining wasn't launched in the Cassleman, Youghiogheny and Potomac Valleys of present-day Garrett County until two decades later. Most of the mines were in the George's Creek region of Allegany County.

Unions in the mines came tentatively to Western Maryland with anti-union sentiment initially outweighing union support during an 1894 general mine strike called by the United Mineworkers (formed in 1890). [15]

The initial burst of coal mine unionism was in George's Creek, but the United Mineworkers later extended its influence into nearby Garrett County towns. The wives of coal miners played a pivotal role on both sides of the labor conflicts in Maryland's mines.

In 1894, wives accompanied their husbands to Consolidation Coal Co.'s Eckhart Mine in Allegany County to turn back union strike supporters who were attempting to get miners to walk off the job. [16] Simultaneously, other wives at the Carlos mine stoned miners who were refusing to strike. [17] The involvement of women in the extraction-based economy would lead many to political engagement.

In 1909, the Just Government League, organized by Baltimore resident Edith Houghton Hooker, conducted a 12-day hike through Western Maryland, seeking support for women's suffrage. On July 2, 1914, *The Republican* reported that 820 Garrett County women had joined the league, with the coal-mining town of Kitzmiller leading recruitment with 75 members. [18]

The role of women in the county's history is a subject of ongoing inquiry and dialogue. In 2021, Stephen Schlosnagle, author of *Garrett County-A History of Maryland's Tableland* (McClain), reassessed his book's treatment of the county's women. Schlosnagle, a fourth-generation descendant of German immigrants to Accident, referenced his book's many pages devoted to Mesach Browning, the legendary pioneer bear hunter and trapper.

"If I were to write that section today," said Schlosnagle, "I might say, 'Mesach Browning was the husband of a pioneer woman—a woman who educated her children, tended the garden, kept the family together, went to the mill, spun the wool and sewed the clothes, tended the babies, churned the butter and milked the cow, while her husband spent his time out in the woods because he enjoyed hunting."

Kitzmiller's contributions to feminism and labor organizing were accompanied by widespread support and acceptance of the Ku Klux Klan. In the 2000s, a server at Kitzmiller's restaurant, The Coal Bucket, recalled her alarm at finding a Klan robe in a trunk in her grandmother's attic. Her grandmother told her the Klan was there to make sure men in the town "acted right" and said the group "protected" women who were being abused by their husbands.

Rebecca A. DeWitt, a Kitzmiller historian, recounted the Klan history in a pamphlet, *Our History of the Kitzmiller Region*: "Apparently Catholics, Irish and Southern Europeans were welcome to join the Ku Klux Klan in Kitzmiller," wrote DeWitt. Most of the town's Catholics attended St. Vincent's Church across the Potomac in Elk Garden, West Virginia.

The West Virginia parish was so rife with Klan influence that the Catholic diocese shut it down and, in 1929, built a new church, Immaculate Conception in Kitzmiller. The Klan was also prominently represented in a 1925 photo in the Garrett County Historical Society Museum of a parade down Second Street in Oakland.

The Republican, August 20, 1925 reported on a "visit" by fifteen members of the Ku Klux Klan to the "local colored M.E. church," that the paper said was "reorganizing." The article stated: [Klan members] "visited the church during the service and after one of the number had made an address in which he assured those present that the order was not prejudiced toward the colored race but at all times worked to assist them in the upholding of the colored man, made a donation of $25.00." The article concluded: "After a fervent prayer offered by one of the Klansmen, the visitors left the church in the same mysterious manner in which the body had entered ten or fifteen minutes before."

As a section of the county's working families weighed the benefits of unionism, Garrett County's cultural elites—many of them part-time residents and tourists—came together in Mountain Lake Park—adjacent to Oakland. Developed by Methodist ministers and business owners from Wheeling, the community enjoyed its lake that Garrett had built to provide winters' ice to B&O passengers and visitors to the company's hotels.

The community became a renowned Chautauqua locale, featuring guest speakers and cultural productions. The leaders and residents of the Mount Lake Park Association inhabited spacious homes on heavily treed lots, welcoming passengers from 13 B&O passenger trains daily until the association's demise in the early 1900s. [19]

Coal miners, loggers and their families faced extreme economic upturns and reversals before and between the world wars. Prior to WWI, the Miner's Relief Fund of 1910 became the first publicly-sponsored relief program in Garrett County. [20]

In 1921, the Youghiogheny Hydro-Electric Corp., a subsidiary of the Pennsylvania Electric Corp. of Johnstown, was granted rights to begin buying land to build a lake in Garrett County. In two years, the company purchased nearly 8,000 acres of land from local farmers and landowners. In 1925, the power company finished its project, Deep Creek Lake, the state's largest lake and, later, the center of Garrett County's tourism industry.

Note: Research into the history of the lake and county tourism is ongoing. In his 2024 online blog, "Dimesey's Domain," Garrett County resident Chris Nichols lists plans and features that preceded the lake's development: In 1824, James Shriver, an engineer with the C&O Canal Co., was asked to investigate building a dam on Deep Creek containing tunnels and canals to connect the lake with the Potomac River on the east and the Cheat River on the west. The project was never begun. In 1883, Gus Delawder, the county's first fish commissioner and T. Harrison Garrett, son of John W. Garrett, purchased 1,000 acres and constructed a dam on Deep Creek where Cherry Creek enters, creating a lake about a mile by one-quarter-of-a-mile wide. Named Lake Cleveland, the body of water was stocked with fish and had canoes available for tourists. In 1892, R.T. Browning, the grandson of Meshach Browning, constructed another dam on Deep Creek near the current Glendale Bridge. Lake Brown, named for the current governor, was stocked with fish and open for public fishing.

[1] Stephen Schlosnagle, *Garrett County, A History of Maryland's Tableland*. Reprint, (Parsons, WV: McClain, 1978), p.300.
[2] Schlosnagle, p. 338
[3]"Indigenous Peoples of Garrett County," Garrett College, https://garrettcolleg.libguides.com/gcindigenouspeoples/home.
[4] WHILBR-Western Maryland's Historical Library (digital.whilbr.org)
[5] Lynn Bowman, *Everyone counts. A history of African American enslavement in Allegany county, Maryland*. (self-published)
[6] Schlosnagle, p. 218
[7] Schlosnagle, p. 214
[8] Schlosnagle, p. 210
[9] Schlosnagle, p. 216
[10] George Cowgill, *Another Visit to the Mountaintop: A History of Mountain Lake Park, Maryland 1881-1921*: (Columbia, S.C.: Big Pasture Publishing, LLC, 2023), 74
[11] Cowgill, p. 77
[12] Cowgill, p. 78
[13] Eugene L. Meyer, *Maryland Lost and Found*, (Centreville, Md: Tidewater, 1986), p. 271
[14] *The Union Comes to Covington: Virginia Paperworkers Organizing 1933-1952*, Robert Zeiger-Proceedings of the American Philosophical Society Vol. 126, No. 1 (Feb. 26, 1982) pp. 51-89
[15] Katherine A. Harvey, *The Best-Dressed Miners-Life and Labor in the Maryland Coal Region* 1835-1910 (Ithaca:Cornell, 1969).
[16] Harvey, p. 283

[17] Harvey, p, 285
[18] Hannah Upole, "Freedom, Fashion and Fundamental Rights: The Suffragette Movement in Western Maryland," The Glades Star, Garrett County Historical Society, Vol. 14. No. 13, March 2021.
[19] Schlosnagle, p. 295
[20] Schlosnagle, p. 293

4

THE NEW DEAL

With the Great Depression came the New Deal, public works projects and fresh attempts by workers to organize. The Garrett County Welfare Board was formed in 1933. By July of that year, 25 percent of the population of the county was living on public assistance. [1]

One member of the Garrett County Board of Commissioners always served on the Welfare Board. The commissioners' influence was significant, as they determined who was eligible for relief or work, directly hiring all county employees.

Garrett County was home to 23 separate New Deal projects, including seven camps of the Civilian Conservation Corps and Public Works Administration projects building roads, residential streets, and parks. Program participants helped build Herrington Manor State Park, New Germany State Park and Oakland Golf Course.

In 1935, the Wagner Labor Relations Act helped incubate new union organizing campaigns. The influence of the United Mineworkers on the job and in local politics spread to Garrett County towns Kitzmiller and Shallmar, both located on the North Branch of the Potomac River.

George Brady, a resident of Shallmar, recounted his father's involvement in the organizing of Wolf Den Coal Co. in a 1991 oral history project conducted by Gail N. Herman, PhD, a Garrett Community College instructor.

Brady described the company's resistance to organizing, including mounting machine guns in the town to intimidate organizers and threatening union supporters with eviction from company-owned houses. He underscored the role of women in "mine country."

Brady recalled a strike at Shallmar (the town's name a reverse spelling of Howard Marshall, owner of Wolf Den Mining Co.) in the 1940's during which a non-union mine in adjacent Kitzmiller continued to operate. The unorganized company attempted to send its coal to West Virginia across a bridge over the Potomac River. A group of strikers blocked the bridge with their vehicles. One of the Kitzmiller company's drivers got out and pointed a double-barrel, sawed-off shotgun at the strikers.

Brady said a woman, one of his neighbors, "ran up to the man, opened her jacket up and threw her breast right up against the shotgun and told them if they wanted to shoot someone, shoot her." [2] The bravery of the coal wars was matched by the sacrifices of county members in the fight against fascism.

More than 2,000 Garrett County citizens fought in WWII, while others remained at home to mine coal for the war effort. The end of the war severely hit Garrett County's miners. By 1950, with the war's booming demand for coal dissipated, many of the mines had shut down for good.

The economic pain was famously represented by the story of Shallmar where, during Christmas, 1949, residents were rescued from starvation by an outpouring of financial support from every U.S. state and other countries as well. [3]

Two years later, the United Mine Workers launched an unsuccessful effort to organize the Banner Mine in Crellin, just outside of Oakland. In the *History of Crellin, Maryland,* author and Oakland resident Robert C. Shaffer wrote: "According to an [April 1951] newspaper account, 'About 400 members of the United Mineworkers battled a three-inch snowfall, icy roads and wintry gales yesterday as the District 31 [UMW] motorcade again went into action to halt operations at Banner Mine #1 on the W.Va./Md. line.'"

Shaffer wrote that the "cat and mouse game" between the United Mine Workers and the company continued through the spring of 1951.

"In the end," he wrote, "The company was victorious. The Union finally gave up the chase, and the Company mines remained non-union to the very end." Banner Mine #1 closed in 1956.

40

Political Party Divide

Kitzmiller's George Brady and other members of his family were staunch and respected Democrats. Maurice Brookhart Sr., a founder of the Garrett County Democratic Club, played the same role in Oakland.

Born in 1915 in Forest Hill, Harford County, Maryland, Brookhart was unemployed during the Great Depression and moved to Garrett County in the mid-1930s to work in the CCC camp at Big Savage Mountain. Brookhart married the daughter of a prosperous Garrett County farmer, moved to Oakland, and enlisted in the U.S. Navy. Upon his return he opened a profitable garage, partnering with local resident Claude Stanton. Brookhart became the vice president of Garrett National Bank, served on the county school board in the late 1950s, and ran a losing campaign for state senate in the 60s.

"I think my dad was a strong Democrat because Franklin Delano Roosevelt saved him [from poverty]," said Brookhart's son, Maurice Brookhart, Jr. "He was a generous man and a bit of a character who tended to loan money to people who were down and out.

"Amusingly, my mother, Martha Engle Brookhart, was a Republican," said Brookhart Jr. A graduate of Western Maryland College, Mrs. Brookhart taught school for a time and worked for the county's social services board.

Despite the widespread support from FDR's New Deal that sustained Brookhart and other Garrett County residents, and despite the administration's support for organized labor, Garrett County remained Republican territory.

Dave Beard was hired in the late 1960s to teach and coach sports at Southern High School in Garrett County. A leader of the teachers' union, he ran losing campaigns for county commissioner as a Democrat, switched his party registration and won a seat.

Beard credited the Republican dominance in the county to Lincoln's assassination and the agrarian influence in the county. "This county was established after the Lincoln assassination [1865]," said Beard. "Tempers were still running high. Lincoln supported the farmers. Farmers are small business people. Conservative Republicanism here is not just a political thing. It's a cultural phenomenon."

Work in the 1950s

One thousand Garrett County farmers were listed on the U.S. Census in 1950, tilling 170 square miles of land. With the demise of coal, new industries sought to tap the natural and human resources of Garrett County, including the work ethic and skills of farmers as both producers and maintenance workers.

In 1958, Douglas Boat Co. began operations, earning worldwide renown with production of the Flying Scot sailboat.

Integrated Business Methods Inc. (IBMI) purchased the facilities of Glenn Engineering in 1965, opening a data processing center that employed large numbers of residents, mostly women, transferring data onto cards and tapes.

Christa Wildeson worked as a keypuncher at IBMI in the 1960s before pursuing a career as a registered nurse. She recalled trucks delivering papers to the plant for clients like National Geographic Magazine. The plant ran on three shifts. "I worked from 10:30 p.m. to 6:30 a.m.," said Wildeson. "I hated midnight shift, but it allowed me to attend nursing school," she said. "We got paid by the keystroke," said Wildeson, who remembers spikes of work during tax season for customers like Riggs Bank in D.C., followed by furloughs during which workers would collect unemployment benefits.

The dominant regional narrative portrayed Cumberland as the "union town" and Garrett County as "anti-union" turf. Cumberland was home to the large Celanese textile plant, Kelly-Springfield Tires and PPG (Pittsburgh Plate Glass) Industries. The unions in those plants had helped to sustain a strong Democratic Party and a working class-oriented political presence, much different from neighboring towns to the west. Union shops were present in Garrett County, too, albeit often much less vocal and assertive than their Allegany County counterparts. So much so, that some residents of the county didn't know they existed.

The coal-rich Allegheny Plateau also held abundant reserves of clay, suitable for manufacturing refractory brick. In 1944, the Union Firebrick Co. opened operations near Jennings, producing firebrick for the steel and glass industries in Pittsburgh and Cleveland, and export to Europe.

District 50 of the United Mine Workers organized the shop, along with two other refractories in Mt. Savage and Zilhman. In 1953, the Flushing Shirt Manufacturing Co. opened a uniform factory in Grantsville. The shop was organized by the International Ladies Garment Workers Union.

Sterling Processing

In 1957, J.W. Ruby opened Sterling's chicken processing plant in Oakland. The plant killed and packaged chickens brought to the location, mostly from farms in nearby West Virginia. Born in 1924 and raised on a farm, J.W. Ruby had gone to work at age 21 in the plating department of Sterling Specialty Co. in Newcomerstown, Ohio. Before WWII, the company transferred Ruby to Morgantown, West Virginia to manage Sterling Faucet Co., which occupied an abandoned mill. Ruby ended up buying the business and became a powerful regional business leader, investing in agriculture, mining, road building, poultry processing, feed mills and racehorses.

One year after Sterling Processing opened, Ruby signed contracts with the Meat Cutters and the Teamsters, covering production workers and truck drivers in the plant.

"I started working at Sterling Processing in 1960," said Helen Tasker, a Kitzmiller resident. "It was hard work. But I liked it. Some people couldn't handle the smell. The only time I noticed the smell was on Monday mornings. We wore rubber boots and rubber aprons. I clipped the gizzards. The lady beside me would take the heart and liver. Government inspectors would come in. We had two lines running."

"Our money all went to J.W. Ruby in Morgantown," said Jerry Sanders, who began weighing and packing chickens at Sterling in 1959. "We went out on strike in 1959 and went back to work for a nickel an hour" more. "[Later] they laid a bunch of us off and we went to work in the coal mines."

Overall, private industry unions were powerful, returning solid gains to their members. But public worker collective bargaining was still in its infancy in the U.S. in the 1950s. The National Labor Relations Act, passed in 1935, had provided protection for workers organizing unions in private industry. But the act excluded those who worked for governmental entities. Protracted legal battles ensued across the nation over the right of public workers to organize and strike.

Steady Work on the Roads

Stable jobs on the county's roads were a desirable alternative after the drastic post-war decline of the area's coal industry, where many workers had increased their wages and benefits as members of the United Mine Workers.

The resilience of and necessity for road workers was driven by nature. Geography was destiny. The county's farms, homes, enterprises, roads, and bridges often faced extreme snowfalls and ice storms, powered by the convergence of up to three climate formations—the Alberta Clipper from Canada, "lake effect" from the Great Lakes and "Nor'easters" from the Atlantic Coast. Road workers, like the miners and loggers before them, kept the county moving through all its seasons and adversities.

In 1957, one week after President Dwight D. Eisenhower was inaugurated for a second term, the Garrett County road workers took their first tentative steps to organize. In the two decades leading to the Garrett Road Workers Strike of 1970, road workers and their supervisors were hired by the county on the recommendation of the commissioners, who divided their patronage to staff garages in Grantsville, Accident, Oakland, and a quarry at Sang Run.

Said one road worker, "They [commissioners] would not let an unmarried guy work on the county roads. If you asked for a job with the roads and wasn't married, you didn't get the job."

With road workers and their managers owing their jobs to individual commissioners, it was natural for their first organizing efforts to include managers and rank and file workers, both seeking the approval of the county's commissioners for more pay, benefits, and respect.

The Garrett County Road Employees' Association

By 1958, 185,000 public workers had joined the American Federation of State, County and Municipal Employees (AFSCME), a union with roots in the white-collar sector. Through aggressive organizing, seventy percent of the union's membership was now blue-collar. But, even as AFSCME had expanded, blue-collar workers—like those in Garrett County—had formed hundreds of local associations, leaving them ripe for later affiliation with a national organization. [4]

The January 30, 1957 minutes of the Board of Commissioners of Garrett County details a meeting with the newly formed Garrett County Road Employees' Association. The association was represented by Theodore Knotts, Franklin Glaze, Kenneth Hetrick, John Filsinger, Gordon Sanders and Road Supervisor, Paul DeWitt. The group presented its constitution and bylaws to the commissioners for approval.

The minutes outline the association's request of both workers and managers to "get the road department employees operation on a system, which has not been done previously."

The workers requested a "sufficient salary raise to make the five nine-hour-a-day pay equal to their present salary for six days." The county road's engineer cautioned that the request would result in a $65,000 per year increase in payroll costs.

A discussion ensued about overtime hours. The parties agreed that rather than hold to a strict 9-hour day, it would "be feasible" for workers who needed a few more hours to complete their assignments to stay on the job, compensated by being assigned shorter hours on succeeding days.

Road workers further asked for a seniority system, ten vacation days, five days sick leave and five paid holidays.

In response to a question from Commissioner Swartzentruber, Theodore Knotts, the association's president, said foremen would be considered members of the association, but could not serve in executive positions. Association members and commissioners agreed that foremen should, for efficiency and continuity, each be responsible for maintenance of specific sections of roads.

The commissioners approved the association's constitution and accepted an invitation to attend the association's next meeting at the volunteer fire hall in Accident.

First Agreement

On April 8, 1958, the Board of County Commissioners, composed of A.C. Brenneman, H.D. Swartzentruber and E.A. Roth, met in special session with eleven representatives of the Garrett County Road Employees' Association and their attorney, C.C. Nathan of Cumberland.

John Filsinger, recruited to the roads department for his respected mechanical skills, served on the association's executive committee. Filsinger and his co-workers requested a 10-cent-per-hour increase in wages; four additional paid holidays; five additional days of leave; one additional day of vacation for each year of service over 10 years, but no vacation to exceed 15 days. They also sought 10 cents per mile – three cents more than workers were getting to use their own vehicles for transportation to jobs; Saturday and Sunday to be paid days in case of emergency, but the work week to remain at 45 hours per week.

The commissioners, serving the last year of their term, told the association the taxes for 1958 had already been levied. While the commissioners deferred all bargaining issues to the incoming commission, they nevertheless voted on a counteroffer.

The commissioners offered no increase in salary; three additional paid holidays; 10 days sick leave not to accumulate over 15 days at any one time; no increase in mileage; nine hours on Saturday and Sunday, only in case of a roads' emergency; and no increase in vacation time.

On April 28, the association's spokesperson, Glen Humberson, requested, once again, the county agree to a 10-cent-per-hour increase. The parties ended up agreeing to a four cent increase, 3 additional holidays, 10 days of sick leave and no increase in vacations. The first agreement was settled.

Successive Agreements

Following the initial contract in 1958, the association and the commissioners negotiated every one or two years. Wage and benefit increases were small, but steady. Succeeding commissioners, however, continued to balk at the establishment of a seniority system.

Many years, full agreements were not reached. The commissioners accepted some of the association's proposals and instituted others on their own terms. Commission minutes often leave out the specifics.

In 1958, the "Eisenhower Recession," an eight-month-long worldwide economic downturn, challenged the road workers' hopes for steady improvements. One year later, with unemployment still high for workers not employed by the county, the Garrett County Department of Social Services offered $10 grocery orders to those unemployed workers in return for one day of work on the county roads.

Men lined up to take advantage of the food assistance. Four months later, a group of the emergency grocery assistance recipients asked the commissioners to grant them the same pay for their time working on the roads as regular employees. The commissioners told them: "It [the work for food plan] was just an effort to help you out. If you don't want to work, you don't have to." (County Commission Minutes, May 18, 1959).

In March 1959, the association requested a discussion on a new contract after the county put all foremen in the association on a salaried schedule. One month later, maintaining its dissatisfaction with the commissioners' proposals on a new agreement, the association asked to continue working under the prior one. Before leaving the table, the commissioners agreed to grant road workers a minimum of 32 hours per week, with a maximum of 40. But the trade-off, they said, might be layoffs for 25 to 30 men.

Association members agreed that, if necessary, *each* member would take a one-month layoff to share the pain. Their counterproposal marked a symbolic step toward deeper organization, weighing the benefits of unity against the whims of their employers.

Comparing Pay Scales

Road workers weren't alone in seeking pay increases from the commissioners. In May, 1959, the Garrett County Teachers Association showed up at a commission meeting asking for pay boosts of $100-a-year per teacher.

Garrett County Secretary of Education Willard Hawkins, a former teachers union leader in both Carroll and Dorchester counties, told the commissioners, "Compared to other teacher salaries, our county is the lowest paid, and their salaries in this county should not be compared with truck drivers, store clerks and others." Hawkins' advocacy encouraged teachers to aspire to more competitive wages and packages while paying closer attention to negotiations in other counties.

Road workers, too, drew comparisons with blue-collar workers in both private industry and state employment. They asked for the "same holidays as the State Highway Commission's employees." The gulf between the benefit and wage packages of county road workers and the more substantial compensation of their peers on the state roads became an issue in each negotiation. The contrasts would grow even sharper after the state workers organized with AFSCME a few years later.

In December 1959, the road association's bargaining committee listed requests for a new agreement. They included a 25-cent-per hour raise, seniority provisions, increased vacation time and improved sick leave.

While the Association sought to address the needs of its members in unison, individual road workers continued to appear before commissioners with their own grievances — men like John Friend, who went before the commissioners June 1960 to appeal his discharge.

The county commission's minutes reveal no further appearances by the Association or references to their contract until the first quarter of 1961.

On Jan. 9, 1961, the commissioners convened a special session to respond to the association's contract demands. The commission's proposal marked a breakthrough for the association. For the first time, the commissioners agreed to a guaranteed 40-hour workweek.

It came with this proviso: "...if there were not sufficient funds in the budget the week could be reduced to 32 or 24 hours until the money was available to return to 40." The guarantee of hours did not prevent the county from sending workers home without pay when it rained.

"My dad was sent home so often due to rain, I thought he had a lot of vacation time," said Lonnie Artice, son of road worker Ray Artice. "Dad would travel five miles into work and he would get sent home," said Tom Holler, son of road worker Lyden Holler.

Jeff Friend, whose father, Ernest Friend, became one of the strike leaders, shares Artice's and Holler's memories. Getting knocked off or told not to report, said the younger Friend, was harsh medicine for a man who, "performed nearly every job in the roads department" and was the kind of guy who was "always ready to help his co-workers, just like he would help neighbors hay their fields or butcher hogs."

The commissioners agreed to a new pay schedule, 13 paid holidays, medical insurance, a grievance procedure, and overtime pay, limited to the first eight hours over 40.

Pay for overtime in lieu of "compensatory time" was a matter of internal controversy. Some road workers wanted to replicate the contracts of their peers at unionized plants in nearby Allegany County, who had won lucrative premium payments for overtime hours. Others, particularly those who farmed, were happy to trade long hours plowing snow in the winter for time off the job during the growing season.

The commissioners included language in the agreement stating: "No competent employee shall be discharged except for a justifiable or reasonable cause."

The "just cause" clause, however, was accompanied by a broad disciplinary edict: "All employees of the Garrett County Roads Department shall conduct themselves in a proper manner in their relationship with each other and with the general public. While on the job, they shall neither use any improper language or conduct, with other employees or the general public. Horseplay shall be strictly forbidden and participants shall be justly punished. Any employee showing disrespect or refusing to obey his foreman, the Supervisors or Assistant Supervisor, shall be subject to discharge."

Finally, the commissioners suggested that salaried supervisors would no longer be members of the Association. Whatever the commissioners' intent, this change resulted in an immediate and longterm change in labor-management relationships. Without supervisors in the ranks, the association now had more in common with the unions that dominated the manufacturing sector in neighboring Allegany County.

The commissioners proposed the contract stay in effect for one year only – January 1961 to December 1961. It lacked a seniority clause but, considering the severe economic situation facing the county, was deemed generous.

[1] Schlosnagle, p. 340

[2] Coal Talk: *Dialogs with people from Western Maryland Coal Communities* (Garrett College, 1991).

[3] James Rada, *Saving Shallmar, Christmas Spirit in a Coal Town.* (Gettysburg: Legacy, 2012).

[4] Joseph E. Slater, *Public Workers, Government Employee Unions, the Law, and the State, 1900-1962* (Ithaca: Cornell, 2004). *164*

5

GROWING PAINS

Public workers suffer the consequences of recession later than private sector workers, but the effects last longer. The Recession of 1960 began in April. National unemployment peaked in May 1961 at 7.1 percent.

Commissioners, under increasing pressure to increase the wages and benefits of road workers and teachers, looked for a way out if they could not find a way forward. While commissioners rarely communicated with state legislators beyond the county's delegate and senator, they now took the extraordinary step of sending a telegram to a newly-elected president of the United States.

John F. Kennedy had campaigned widely in Appalachia, promising aid and attention to education and infrastructure in rural economies. Nevertheless, in the '60 election, Garrett County voters rejected the Kennedy-Johnson ticket in favor of the Nixon-Lodge ticket by a vote of 4,932 to 2,291.

But on Feb. 3, 1961, directly after Kennedy's inauguration, county commissioners Carl Schell (Kitzmiller), Elra Garletts (Friendsville) and Fred Glotfelty (Oakland) sent telegrams to Kennedy with copies to the U.S. Senators Charles Mc C. Mathias, J. Glenn Beall, and Maryland Gov. J. Millard Tawes.

It read: "Unemployment situation and poverty conditions in Garrett County, Maryland critical. County commissioners of Garrett County unanimously request that Garrett County be incorporated into President Kennedy's program for relief for distress areas. Percentage of unemployment is approximately 15%, which is more than double the national average."

Six months after sending the telegram, the three commissioners asked that Garrett County be considered for federal funds from the Area Redevelopment Administration (ARA). The original bill to establish the ARA program, the first to advance economic development by region, had been vetoed by President Eisenhower. Legislative compromises weakened the bill before its passage during the Kennedy administration. By 1963, public facility grants under the redevelopment act were exhausted. No funds had been sent to Garrett County.

Two years later, during President Lyndon Johnson's administration, the Public Works and Economic Development Act was passed, replacing the ARA with the Economic Development Administration (EDA). The county's road workers and local businesses could have benefited from EDA funds focused on improving the basic infrastructure, repairing, or building public water and sewage capacity and roads. Once again, Garrett County received no funds.

In March, 1967, John Moore Jr., a field coordinator from the Economic Development Administration, based in Wilkes-Barre Pennsylvania, convened a meeting with the county commissioners and a group of 12 county residents at Oakland City Hall.

Attending the meeting were Robert Rudy, Patricia H. Kittle, Daniel S.J. Rohrer, Frederic Bartlett, William Nace, Russell Smith, George T. Perrine, Walter Price, Allen Murray, Charles C. Bender, Clinton Englander and Wesley Schaible.

The EDA notified the group that, since 1961, when a prior commission had sent a telegram requesting funds from the Kennedy administration, the county had failed to submit progress reports to qualify for EDA funding. Local parties then committed to follow through on proper protocols to qualify for aid to develop modern sanitation and improved roads.

Were the county commissioners guilty of incompetence in not submitting reports? Or was their call for federal help and their subsequent failure to follow through a reflection of conflicted political opposition to "big government," going back to the New Deal?

County farmers would rarely refuse federal subsidies. Despite their acceptance of help, many farmers and county business leaders criticized government programs assisting workers, the unemployed and the poor, contending they created a culture of "dependence." Within a few years, that charge would be leveled at road workers applying for food stamps after being fired by commissioners for demanding union recognition.

Roads Association Renews Advocacy

During the remainder of 1961, association representatives continued to appear at commission meetings advocating for pay upgrades of individual road workers. Roads supervisors became more vocal in advancing their own status as well.

A rift between a supervisor and the ranks of the association brought the group's attorney, Jack Turney, before the commission in November. Turney argued that Ron Steyer, who had previously served as the association's president, was "holding two jobs" and should remain as a foreman or be "cut back" to an operator's job.

The same month, George DeWitt, the foreman at the Sang Run quarry, threatened to give up his supervisory job if the commissioners didn't hire a welder and additional workers.

In February, 1961, salaried foremen Homer Glotfelty and Ken Hetrick asked for pay upgrades for the roads' department's salaried foremen. The commissioners gave no answer. A month later, attorney Jack Turney returned to the commission to protest the demotion of Owen Bach, one of the founders of the association.

In 1963, the Association presented the commissioners with new contract proposals. The 1962 commission had borrowed $125,000 from local banks to balance the budget. Perhaps it was another tight budget and lean times that led Martin Tichnell, the association's spokesman, to propose a one-year contract with *no* increase in rates of pay.

The Association re-introduced its prior requests for members to be paid for *all* overtime hours worked, a guarantee of 40 hours of work per week and seniority recognized for job selection. The minutes report that, in discussions on the 40-hour guarantee, some raised the question of whether it was "fair to taxpayers" for workers to be paid when it was raining, and they couldn't perform their regular jobs. [The minutes don't reflect if individual commissioners raised those questions or others in attendance at the meeting]. Road workers responded that there was *always* sufficient work to keep them busy during inclement weather.

The Association backed off on any changes in holidays or vacations but requested 30 days of sick leave in lieu of the current 10. They also requested that the position of "craft foreman" be dropped, saying, "all operators shall bear the same classification." The road workers' proposal stripped language from the prior contract that enabled the county to lay off employees and to enforce a mandatory retirement age.

Attorney Turney returned to the commission in July. The minutes state that Turney agreed that all of the issues in a new 1963-1964 agreement had been "resolved" except overtime pay. Once again, the association requested that former association president Ron Steyer's pay be reduced, citing a membership vote in which 36 out of 46 association members supported the reduction.

In the regions' union shops, members would have been scorned for advocating a pay cut for a fellow worker. The Association's request revealed the lack of such discipline or solidarity. The commissioners refused to reduce Steyer's pay.

Association president Tichnell accused commissioners of violating the terms of the agreement by failing to dock Steyer's pay. [Tichnell's protest implies that Steyer was holding the position of "craft foreman" the association was seeking to eliminate].

The commissioners told the representatives they should, "act like gentlemen, let the contract ride as is for this year and present a new contract for 1964 between Nov 15 and Dec. 1."

The county sought to provide roads work to some residents suffering from unemployment and recession. In October 1963, Robert Stemple, director of the county's welfare board, introduced a new program.

Dependent children of welfare recipients would be hired on public jobs, including the roads, with one-half their pay covered by the county, the other paid by the welfare agency. Some of the dependents would be hired for permanent positions. Six months after introducing the program, Stemple complained that no workers in the welfare-to-work program had been hired permanently in the roads department during the previous seven months.

1965 Strike

Sometime during 1965, the roads workers called a one-day strike, a remarkable event for an association with no legal status to collectively bargain for its members.

The parties reached no agreement in 1965 negotiations. The commissioners imposed their terms. Perhaps it was the memory of the one-day strike the same year that led the commissioners to order DeWitt to post a warning in the garages stating: "All men are urged to report to work on July 7, 1965 at regular time. Those not complying may be subject to dismissal." In May, 1966, the commissioners granted the roads workers a 10-percent increase—the first general wage boost since 1960.

One month earlier, the commission instituted a new medical insurance plan covering all hourly and salaried roads workers. The plan increased costs for roads workers amounting to a maximum of $1.92 per pay for family coverage. In August, the Association requested a meeting with the commissioners to discuss the medical care cost hikes.

Representing the association were Emory DeWitt, Ronald Weimer, LeRoy Friend, Lawrence Lewis, Milton Savage, John Tasker, and Jack Sowers. The group asked the county to cover the increased out-of-pocket insurance costs, contending the county could then make up some of the cost by applying any dividends received on insurance to the county treasury. Since the year's tax levy had already been established, the issue was referred to the next county budget deliberations.

While some progress had been made over the previous decade on wages and benefits, winning seniority and pay for overtime in lieu of compensatory time continued to evade the association.

"To get a good job [a promotion], you still had to know the right person. You had to go see a commissioner," said Jim Fike, who was hired on the roads in 1962, but recalled pay so low he needed to work a second job to make ends meet.

Road workers understood commissioners had a responsibility to spend tax monies wisely. But the men who threw cinders from the back of trucks in sub-zero weather and their drivers, who deftly kept their trucks from sliding off icy hills, continued to demand premium pay for overtime.

Memphis Sanitation Strike Spurs National Organizing

The Memphis sanitation strike of 1968, that pivotal clash of race and class, had thrust the American Federation of State County and Municipal Employees into the national limelight. In the wake of Dr. Martin Luther King's assassination, AFSCME organizers were continuing to win battles across the U.S. to affiliate their union with hundreds of local associations of public workers.

Estimates put the number of new AFSCME members at 1,000 a week during 1969. Some of the growth came through mergers with populous state and county employee groups, including the New York Civil Service Association and the Hawaii Government Employees Association. [1]

We Got to the Place Where We Needed a Little Backing

In 1969, three Garrett County roads' department workers, members of the Association, traveled to the Western Maryland Central Labor Council's office in Cumberland. They met with organizers from AFSCME to begin planning a campaign for affiliation. A participant in the meeting said the men in the room swore to never disclose who was there.

Despite signing successive three-year agreements, by 1969, many of the association's original goals were still unmet. Overtime pay and seniority were nagging concerns, but so was pay. Notwithstanding regular increases, pay was so low that—as many of the road workers would later find out—they could have qualified for food stamps.

While the original organizers can't be identified, the ranks of men who quickly came to support their call revealed a breadth of experience in work and war.

Johnny Tasker was hired by the roads department in 1960. "We [roads workers] got to the place where we needed a little backing," said Tasker, a resident of Sang Run, who was born in 1933 in Vindex, Md., the mining town on the Potomac River. Tasker had gone to work full-time at age 16. His father, a former coal miner, was unable to work because of the effects of gas poisoning he suffered during World War I.

Harold Riggleman was born in Vindex in 1930. Like his grandfather, he began working in the area's mines. "My dad told me he hated work in the mines," said his daughter Shari Riggleman Whetstone. Riggleman joined the Army but was caught slipping through underage and released. He came back to Garrett County, went back briefly to the mines, and got a job on the roads.

Joy Dale Sweitzer Sr., born in 1928 on a farm in Swanton, was the son of a B&O Railroad worker. Sweitzer began working on the county roads in 1948 as a laborer, then worked as a mechanic, a blacksmith and grader operator. "My dad worked the night shift for the county and then ran 'dozers, front-end loaders and backhoes for B&E Construction Co. during the day," said Joy Dale Sweitzer Jr. "He lost one eye [on the county roads' job] when a piece he was welding on blew up."

Sweitzer Sr. worked 40 years on the roads. "My dad taught me to respect people," said Sweitzer Jr., one of eight children who grew up in Mountain Lake Park. "And I was his right-hand man on mechanical work," said Sweitzer Jr., who bought a few lathes after he graduated high school and worked alongside his father fabricating tools for Amish farmers in nearby Pleasant Valley.

Dominic Pratt was the son of Italian immigrants who had arrived in Ellis Island. "Their name was Prato, but it was changed to Pratt at Ellis Island," says Dominic Pratt's niece, Rosalie Finch, daughter of Fred J. Pratt, a Kitzmiller miner and member of the United Mineworkers.

Dominic Pratt retired as a coal miner before being hired at the county roads department. "He could build anything," said his nephew, Paul Pratt, a retired deputy sheriff. "My uncle didn't have a formal education. He was a hands-on kind of guy. He was thrifty and if something needed doing, he did it himself," said Paul Pratt. Dominic Pratt used his savings to buy snowmobiles and vacation in Ocean City, Md. and in Northern Michigan. Active in Democratic Party politics, he purchased land on Harvey's Peninsula, on the north shore of Deep Creek Lake, and was known as the "mayor" of the peninsula.

Leo Miller was hired in 1966. Born to a farm family in the Garrett County sawmill town of Jennings, he had completed Army service in Germany during the Korean War and returned home. But looking for steady work, Miller headed for Cleveland where he was employed for a time in union-organized industrial plants. Longing for home and family, Miller returned to Garrett County and was working on the family farm when he started at the roads department. Not long after his hiring, he was elected as a representative of the Association.

Strikers Eugene and Victor Nazelrod Sr. from Deer Park, outside of Oakland, were second-generation roads workers. Their father, John Nazelrod was a roads foreman, a member of the Association and a former county commissioner who retired before the organizing drive. He and his wife, Ellen Self Nazelrod, had four daughters and seven sons, all of whom served in the armed forces. One son, Pvt. Calvin Nazelrod, was killed in action in WWII in 1944.

"My daddy went to work for the roads before WWII and was then drafted," said Curtis Nazelrod, Eugene Nazelrod's son. Eugene Nazelrod sustained injuries twice in the Philippines and on Okinawa, one injury the result of friendly fire from Navy bombs dropped too close to his unit. "He had shrapnel up and down his back and was missing the tip of one of his fingers," said his son. Returning from the service, Eugene Nazelrod went back to work on the roads, running a bulldozer. "They said if a man wanted to get a shave from a 'dozer, my daddy could do it," said his son, recalling his father being offered a job as a demonstrator for a bulldozer manufacturing company.

In one demo for Caterpillar, Eugene Nazelrod took a cigar out of a man's mouth with the bulldozer and put it back with a clam bucket. In 1972, after suffering damage to his kidneys, Eugene Nazelrod went to work in the blacksmith's shop, making chains, plow shoes and other equipment alongside J.D Sweitzer. He retired five years later.

Eugene Nazelrod had worked, in his youth, in a CCC camp at the site of today's Swallow Falls State Park, said another son, John Nazelrod. He remembered his dad leaving home early for the 7:00 a.m. starting time for his shift at the garage, driving a 1952 Chevrolet pick-up truck slower than Oakland's speed limit. "Dad knew what you needed to know," said John Nazelrod, who said his father directed his mother, his brother and him in building their home. "We used to wire houses, me and my dad, before we needed licenses," said John Nazelrod.

Victor Nazelrod was a truck driver. Victor Nazelrod Jr. said, "My dad knew the county commissioners could just say they didn't like someone [working on the roads] and get them fired." Nazelrod Jr. later worked for 31 years as a heavy equipment mechanic and AFSCME member on the state roads. He said, "Before the union, the county didn't want nothing to do with people making more money or having seniority on the job. If you didn't know the right people in town, you were out of luck."

A striker who chose to remain anonymous says one of the reasons for organizing was: "[hiring and promotions] were a 'family affair.' Every good [job] that came along [in the garage where he worked], a family member got it."

While many of the strikers grew up on farms or worked on them in their youth, their experience in military service or in private industry inspired a wider understanding of the need for workers to speak with one voice, with or without unions.

Don Colaw Sr. had tried unsuccessfully to organize his fellow KRAY coal miners into the United Mineworkers. Dozens of others had industrial experience in and beyond Garrett County. Asa Wilhelm worked for Celanese textiles in Allegany County. Berman Butler, hired on the roads in 1954 at age 21, had previously worked in a steel mill in Cleveland. Lyden Holler had been a coal miner in Kempton and Vindex. Rodger Evans worked at Sterling Processing.

The roads department hired Calvin "Leo" Rinker in 1958. "My dad graduated from Bruceton, WV High School. If they had scouts come out, he probably would have been a professional pitcher," said his son, Terry.

Instead, Rinker entered the service and landed on the Belgian

59

front. A tanker commander sergeant, he was on his walkie-talkie when a mortar hit his tank. He took seven pieces of shrapnel in his left arm and shoulder. "He wouldn't talk about the war much," said his son. Leo tried farming before being hired at the Celanese textile mill in neighboring Allegany County.

The mill had a militant history. Rinker's predecessors had engaged in strikes and sit-ins to win recognition of the Textile Workers union. George Meyers, a native of Lonaconing in Allegany County, a spinner at Celanese and a member of the U.S. Communist Party, was an early president of the 13,000-member Textile Workers Local 1874.

"My dad was a hard worker who didn't take crap out of anyone," said Terry Rinker. He was 5'9" and 270 lbs. He'd tell guys he was having trouble with [on the job] he'd take them out behind the garage. But he'd do anything for anybody. One day, somebody's car broke down on front of his house. He replaced a hose on the vehicle."

Political, Economic Changes Spur Organizing

In the presidential primary election of 1968, the Richard Nixon-Spiro Agnew (Republican Party) ticket garnered 59 percent of the Garrett County vote. The Hubert Humphrey-Edmund Muskie (Democratic Party) ticket won 28 percent and the George Wallace-Curtis LeMay (American Independent Party) ticket received 12 percent.

The county's population had grown to nearly 22,000. But, by 1970, the number of farmers in Garrett County had fallen from one thousand in 1950 to 415.

Garrett County's median per capita income of $11,632 was dramatically lower than the state's $21,850. A 1969 map shows nearly the entire county living 20 or more percent below the poverty level except for those inhabiting the mercantile center in Oakland and Mountain Lake Park and the communities of Avilton and Bloomington, adjacent to the heavy, unionized industry of Allegany County. [2]

Western Maryland's mining industry shifted its focus from the deep mines of Allegany County to the strip mines of Garrett County. The DelSignore and Nethken families and other owners employed

60

only about 200 workers in strip-mines, all of them unorganized. Both wealthy mine-owning families were noted for their private planes and other symbols of wealth. But, with few private schools nearby, many of their sons and daughters attended the same schools with sons and daughters of the blue-collar working class.

The cross-class relationships that were built helped encourage residents on either end of the income ladder to coalesce, fighting for good schools and educational achievement. Land prices were still low. A new generation of builders, real estate and tourism entrepreneurs and better-trained farmers was building wealth and influence.

Garrett County's public-school teachers were encouraged by freshly won state-sanctioned collective bargaining rights. Legislative efforts to win bargaining for other state, county and municipal employees had failed in the state legislature. Garrett County's teachers split their allegiances between the National Educational Association and the American Federation of Teachers. "I was the charter vice president of the AFT when it was formed in 1968," said subsequent Garrett County Commissioner and teacher Dave Beard. "We split from the Garrett County Teacher's Association (NEA). We thought they were too weak. We were AFT-AFL-CIO."

Anti-Union Employers Dominate Local Economy

The most powerful and influential locally owned businesses in Garrett County, most of the county commissioners and the editor of *The Republican,* George Hanst, were all "decidedly anti-union," said James R. "Smokey" Stanton, a sixth-generation Garrett County resident and a former president of the Oakland City Council.

Retailers A.D. Naylor (hardware and appliances), the Browning family (groceries) and the Felds, owners of the HP Stores chain (clothing), controlled the local banks and steered money to like-minded entrepreneurs.

"The thinking was, if a union came in during this window of time between 1965 and 1975, it would hurt existing businesses," said Stanton. There was, he said an effort by some business leaders to bring in a VA hospital to complement the care offered by Garrett

County Memorial Hospital. "It was opposed because it would have increased labor costs, even though it might have grown economic development," said Stanton.

Harry Biggs, a teacher at Southern High School in Oakland who retired in 2024, worked for Browning's Foodland as a bag packer and moved up, becoming the company's human resources director. The store faced a union organizing campaign in the 1960s. The Browning family hired a labor consultant to fend off the union.

The consultant told the owner's sons to get their father out of the store," said Biggs, because his management style was the reason folks had turned to a union. The drive was defeated.

"There were two tiers of pay in the county," often defined by gender and broadly accepted, said Biggs. "If you asked a man at Browning's if he deserved more money he would say, 'Yes.' But if you asked him about his wife, who worked as a cashier, he would say 'No.'"

Don "Toby" Colaw Jr., the son of striker Don Ray Colaw Sr., graduated from Southern High School in 1956 and went to work for Browning's. After contacting organizers from the Retail Clerks union in Cumberland, he attempted to sign up his co-workers, seeking better pay and benefits. Stuck in his craw was a decision he deemed to be a personal affront from the owners. In 1960, his 12-year-old sister died, and he took four days off. One of the owner's sons told him he wouldn't receive any pay but could "make up" the days. "I was down to two hours [make up time] and he cut me off," said Colaw.

"The 'union buster' [from Tennessee] brought his bodyguard with him," said Colaw. The outsiders, he said, put his apartment in downtown Oakland under surveillance. "[One of the Brownings] told me he heard I was talking about a union," said Colaw. "He said if I kept doing that, he would let me go." Colaw quit.

The wife of one of Colaw's co-workers at Brownings worked as a telephone operator at C&P Telephone Co., serving for a time as a shop steward for the union representing the operators. Her husband was fired during the organizing campaign. She helped him file a complaint with the National Labor Relations Board.

She remembers one of the Browning sons showing up at her door after the charge was filed, saying he tossed an envelope at her containing money he owed her husband. The organizing defeat at Browning's was a "turning point in the town," she said. "I stood outside Browning's [after the union's loss] and said to myself, 'We will never see decent wages paid here.'"

Smokey Stanton noted the distinct cultural differences between the mostly rural Northern end of Garrett County and the more business-oriented and suburban areas to the south. But, he said, farmers and most small business owners often had a "meeting of the minds on many issues, including taxes and [opposition to] unions." And farmers had no choice but to maintain the closest relationships with the banks and their directors to secure credit, especially during lean years.

It took skilled leaders like B.O. Aiken, a Democrat, to bridge the cultural and economic gaps within the county and win some support in Annapolis.

Delegate B.O. Aiken

B.O. Aiken, born in 1899, was one of 12 children of a North Carolina tobacco farmer whose father had owned slaves. After playing football at Trinity College (now Duke University), Aiken moved to Chicago to get his master's in education.

Graduating amidst the 1929 stock market crash, he found work teaching in Poolesville in Montgomery County, Md. He later moved to Accident.

After serving 20 years as principal in Accident's elementary school, Aiken retired and began making house calls to teach students who were homebound. In 1966 Aiken, a Democrat, won a seat in the Maryland House.

"My dad thought we needed Garrett College in part to attract businesses like Bausch and Lomb, [which relocated to Garrett County from Rochester, N.Y. in 1970]. He fought to build the college despite legislation that barred community colleges in adjoining counties," said Bill Aiken, B.O. Aiken's son.

The elder Aiken fended off concerns of many local businesses and farmers who complained that Bausch and Lomb's presence would unrealistically drive wages up for county-based businesses. He consistently advocated for the needs of local businesses and the farm community, said his son.

"B.O. Aiken was a great guy," said lifelong Republican Tom Bernard. "I thought he stood head and shoulders over a lot of people. I looked up to people who were successful. He struck me as being informed. Anytime I had an interaction, he seemed to be [very] reasonable."

Owning property atop a rich natural gas field, Aiken enhanced his civic reputation by organizing a group of landowners to bargain for the most desirable leases from Texas Eastern for the natural gas reserves.

Exploitation of the county's natural gas resources had begun in 1951, when two-dozen natural gas derricks were placed in Mountain Lake Park, adjoining Oakland. Snee and Eberly Gas Co., Texas Eastern's predecessor, drilled their first natural gas well near Accident in 1953.

In 1963, Texas Eastern announced plans to build a major storage site in Accident. The company said many of the wells had been drawn out. Aiken showed up at a commission meeting as spokesman for a group of Accident residents, Mitchell Resh, Walter Harman, Claudine Friend and [Mr.] Beachy. Aiken questioned the commissioners about how Texas Eastern's plans would affect both the county's tax base and the leases of individual property owners. Lewis Jones, the county's attorney, also represented Texas Eastern, telling the group he was "in a spot," advising them to get their own attorney.

Within a decade, Texas Eastern's wells, averaging a depth of 7,375 feet, were filling the Accident Dome, an underground storage space of 34,000 acres. It was the first completely automated storage field in the gas industry. [3]

"My dad's involvement with Texas Eastern really helped him politically," said Bill Aiken, who further stated B.O. and his group did hire an attorney as advised, and succeeded in boosting lease payments—even for residents who had been pressured earlier into signing less advantageous contracts.

Aiken positioned himself as a conservative Democrat, opposing more liberal state party leaders on issues like gun regulation.

During his term, he helped win lower tax assessments for farmers' livestock and farm machinery and lower property taxes on the homes of the elderly. He supported legislation for better salaries and retirement benefits for state employees and teachers. And he won approval for installing a sewerage system at Deep Creek State Park. He supported the owners and workers at the Luke, Maryland paper mill and fought for a law to reclaim land disrupted by strip mining.

Garrett County farmers, organized as the Garrett County Maple Industry Assoc., produced three grades of maple syrup. The "fancy" grade was sent to Vermont where it was bottled under well-known brands.

"My dad would fill a truck full of [locally harvested] maple syrup and give bottles to fellow legislators and committee chairs in Annapolis," said Bill Aiken. "And he placed one of his [former] students as secretary to the House Ways and Means Committee. He knew what was going on and how to make things happen."

The Outsider Waves

"In 1970, Garrett County's farmers were having a good year," said Bill Aiken, who, after graduating from West Virginia University, worked for both the Maryland and West Virginia farm bureaus. Aiken said many dairy farms, which have long since ceased operations, were still thriving and crop prices were adequate.

Commercial and retail enterprises serving Garrett County residents were organized in a triangle. Consumers from Kitzmiller and Bloomington, a town near the vast and unionized Westvaco Paper Mill in Luke, Maryland on the Potomac, would shop in Westernport in Allegany County and Piedmont, West Virginia.

Garrett County residents west of those towns and nearby in West Virginia would shop in Oakland. Garrett County residents in the northernmost region might shop in Morgantown, West Virginia, or Cumberland, Maryland and LaVale in Allegany County.

Long before Interstate Rte. 68 cut through to Garrett County, inviting tourists and second-home owners from Washington, Baltimore and Northern Virginia, visitors to Garrett County came from nearby Pennsylvania, including large numbers of workers and managers from Pittsburgh's steel industry.

Most vacationed in modest cabins around 65 miles of Deep Creek Lake shoreline. Famous residents and visitors who enjoyed the natural wonders of Garrett County's streams, rivers, and forests included Albert Einstein, tire magnate Harvey Firestone, and Dr. Jonas Salk, developer of the polio vaccine.

The county always had a complicated relationship with "outsiders." The first wave of "outsiders" to the county, after the white settlers, were the coal and timber capitalists who gave their names to towns like Jennings, Crellin and Shallmar.

Industrialists were soon joined by vacationing homeowners of Mountain Lake Park, a community just east of Oakland that became a center of summer Chautauqua programs, inviting guest speakers and leaders in arts and letters. The Mountain Lake Park Association and Chautauqua began to fade in 1921, but the summer visitors kept returning to the town's spacious Queen Anne and country Gothic cottages. Nearly 150 of the cottages now constitute a National Historic District.

In the late 1950s, the Garrett County Theatre, founded by Gene and Barbara Yell, revisited the cultural influences of the Chautauqua. Gene Yell, a graduate of the University of Chicago's theater school, married fellow graduate, Barbara Burruss, in 1943. Barbara Burruss's parents owned a home, "Hemlock Hollow" in Pleasant Valley, south of Oakland, purchased in 1925.

In 1956, after his hiring as a professor of theater at the University of New Mexico, Gene Yell founded a summer theater, the Garrett County Playhouse, on McHenry Cove on Deep Creek Lake. He recruited influential local citizens to serve on the board, including Irvin Feld, Edward Smouse, and George Littman, and he employed local folks at the venue.

Each summer for 30 years, Yell brought several of his students east to stay in a bunkhouse at Hemlock Hollow. They and their local collaborators produced a play-a-week for eight weeks. After several years of operation, Yell recruited professional actors from New York to join the summer theater for six-week sessions.

66

"The theater was pretty rustic," said Jennifer Yell Kirwan, Barbara and Gene Yell's daughter, born in 1944. "I remember bats flying across the stage."

There was a fire in the theater's original barn in 1962, said Kirwin. "But, the night of the fire, the show still went on at a local high school because of the support Daddy had in town."

Kirwan continued, "My mother was a union girl," noting that Barbara Yell had worked for the International Ladies Garment Workers Union and was involved in the Federal Theatre Project. In her work, she had befriended playwright Noel Coward and Pulitzer Prize winning journalist Studs Terkel. She opened a boutique at the playhouse to sell unique items from her travels in the American Southwest and Mexico.

"My parents developed a lot of close friendships in Garrett County," said Kirwin. Friends included locals, like pharmacist and school board member Clinton Englander, as well as other frequent visitors, including Dr. Jonas Salk, whose sons worked in the theater.

By 1966, Wisp Resort was making its own snow, launching the most sustained boom in tourism and real estate since the building of the luxurious hotels at the turn of the century that had catered to urbane passengers arriving aboard the B&O Railroad.

[1] Francis Ryan, *AFSCME'S Philadephia Story-Municipal Workers and Urban Power in the Twentieth Century*. (Philadelphia: Rutgers, 2011). 189
[2] "Maryland Family Income Characteristics: 1970 Census"- Planning Department, City Hall, Hagerstown, Md.
[3] Schlosnagle, P. 343

6

THE TURBULENT SIXTIES

At first blush, the social and political turmoil of the 1960s largely escaped Garrett County, typified by the story on the front page of *The Republican* about "hippies" being "spotted" in downtown Oakland. But the debate over the nation's political and cultural priorities and the role of "outsiders" in county affairs could not be avoided.

Several years prior to the arrival of "outside" organizers from the AFSCME in Garrett County, Lyndon Johnson's "War on Poverty" encouraged a unique partnership between native-born county residents and outsiders that, like AFSCME, worked at the grassroots.

The 1964 Economic Opportunity Act enabled the establishment of community action agencies across the nation to initiate programs addressing poverty in identified cities and towns.

While monies were available to serve rural communities, the community action framework was initially designed to address the problem of youth gangs in low-income city neighborhoods. Johnson administration members argued that, by involving community members in the planning of social services, educational and vocational programs, "blocked avenues" of opportunity could be opened that would undercut crime and unemployment in urban and rural communities.

Rules were written for urban and rural program recipients that required community action agencies to be led by tripartite boards drawn from the areas' political leadership, business owners and individual members of the community who were being served by the programs.

Community Action was highly debated. As political activists assumed leading positions in many local agencies in urban and rural areas, conflicts developed between them and elected leaders over how federal funds would be allocated.

In Garrett County, Ross Sines attempted to sever the Board of Commissioners' ties to the county's community action committee, saying the agency should be fully funded by federal, not local funds. He could not get a second to his motion. Despite local wariness of federal programs, the Community Action Committee's mission and assistance became broadly accepted in Garrett County. There was no organized opposition to using a percentage of county revenues to supplement federal programs to serve the county's impoverished and unemployed residents with housing and food needs.

Community Action

Founded in 1965, the Garrett County Community Action Committee (GCCAC) developed into a nationally recognized model in service to rural communities. Eighty percent of the agency's funding came from the federal government, twenty from Garrett County.

GCCAC's 15-member board of directors included five members from the low-income community, five members from the general population, and five from county government. Garrett County Republican Commissioner and local farmer Allen S. "Dick" Paugh served on the board alongside Democrat Del. B.O. Aiken.

Garrett County-born residents were at the core of the GCCAC's founding, most notably, Alta Schrock, the renowned educator and community organizer, born in 1911 at Strawberry Hill Farm, near Grantsville. Schrock was the first Mennonite woman in the U.S. to earn a PhD degree. She taught biology at American University and Goshen College in Indiana before returning to Western Maryland in 1960 to teach at Frostburg University.

Ms. Schrock, who later founded the celebrated Penn Alps Center and Spruce Forest Artisan Village, hired Bradford Rinard, a transplant from Kanawha County, West Virginia, to lead the CAC. Smokey Stanton, who was later hired by Rinard to work in alcohol and drug abuse counseling, said Rinard was an "old style anti-poverty community organizer from Charleston [W. Va.]."

Schrock and Rinard asked Lowell Bender to direct a Head Start

69

center in Jennings. Bender, born in 1940, had returned to Garrett County in 1963 after service as a conscientious objector in Europe.

A sociology major at Eastern Mennonite University, Bender joined the Mennonite Central Committee's Alternative to Military Service Program during the early days of the Vietnam War. He worked in Europe for two years, building houses for refugees in the former Yugoslavia.

Upon his return from Europe, Bender met with Robert Stemple, the county's director of social services. Bender helped establish a program utilizing community volunteers to better serve the needs of county residents facing poverty.

Rinard offered to hire Bender as director of community organizing. Weighing the political conservatism of a county that branded community organizers as political "radicals," Bender suggested his job be titled "director of community development." Rinard consented.

In 1972, Bender hired his first cousin, Garrett County native Duane Yoder, to assist CAC's work, upon Yoder's graduation from Eastern Mennonite University. Bender also hired Dave Ramsey, a Beaver County, Pa. native who had just returned with his wife Sara from three years in the Peace Corps, including service in Bolivia.

Bender began putting together a group of canvassers the agency called "neighborhood aides" to work in five areas of the county classified under federal guidelines as "high poverty."

The grassroots, all women neighborhood aides went door-to-door to assess the needs of families in Friendsville, Jennings, Avilton, Crellin and Kitzmiller. The organizing experience helped prepare the women for new roles. One of the aides, Cathy Lyons, a native of Kitzmiller, was elected president of AFSCME Local 1834 after the roads strike.

In addition to Cathy Lyons, neighborhood aides included Vivian Tasker (Kitzmiller), Dolly Livengood (Jennings), Ethel Kelly (Friendsville) and Bernadine Friend (Crellin).

The aides' work was critical in obtaining federal funds to feed residents and seniors and providing housing improvements and transportation needs. Asked about the aides, Duane Yoder said, "Their most interesting stories came from their exposure to the outside world while participating in training, meetings and workshops at national and statewide events."

"We were right on the cusp of Lyndon Johnson's Great Society," said Bender, who later worked at Garrett Community College.

Bender remembered one of the Garrett County aides being assigned to partner with a Black aide in neighboring Allegany County. Both were training in the collection of data. Wary of working with a Black partner, "She [the Garrett County aide] was ready to quit," said Bender. "But they developed a relationship."

The University of Maryland Extension Service also had aides. They were focused on meal preparation and other family support. Health centers in Oakland, Grantsville, Friendsville, Kitzmiller and Bloomington, part of LBJ's "War on Poverty," were bases of operation to additional aides.

"All of these aides absolutely performed a community organizing function and cooperated to serve the needs of their clients," said Smokey Stanton.

GCCAC's growing influence came on the heels of the transition of the Garrett County Welfare Board in the early 1960s into the Garrett County Department of Social Services, under the auspices of the state of Maryland. Some local politicians resented the transition as a state intrusion on the "internal affairs" of the county.

It was against this background of community organizing and political, economic, and cultural ferment—both national and regional—that Garrett County commissioners were now being asked to recognize an aggressive international union. There couldn't have been a starker contrast between an all-white, all-male county association of road workers and AFSCME.

The Garrett County Road Employees Association had been formed in 1957 with the consent and participation of the county commissioners. AFSCME was the union that had just won international notoriety as striking Black sanitation workers carrying signs saying, "I Am A Man" garnered international attention in Memphis, particularly after the assassination of the Rev. Martin Luther King Jr. there during the strike.

Structural Blocks to Collective Bargaining

While community organizers were widely accepted, an intensifying polarization was developing over unions and collective bargaining. The structure of county government contributed to the rift.

In Maryland, counties can opt for one of three separate forms of governance: charter, "code-home rule" or a non-charter Commissioner format. At the time, Garrett County still maintained a non-charter Commissioner form of County government.

Tim Dugan, in his chapter in *Western Maryland: A Profile* (1980), said, "This had the advantages of being familiar and relatively simple, but it also means that the three-member board of County Commissioners has only that authority which is explicitly granted to it by the State General Assembly."

Garrett County's lack of political autonomy was so extreme that commissioners needed approval from the state to change the day of commission meetings. The commission's weak authority had a direct impact on the right of public workers and their unions to engage in collective bargaining.

Maryland had no state law governing the rights of most public employees. Statewide bargaining statutes covered only teachers and non-certificated employees in schools and institutions of higher education.

The principal functions of the Garrett County Board of Commissioners in 1966 were preparing the county budget and tax levy, appointing county employees (nearly all patronage positions), serving as the local Board of Health, maintaining county roads and buildings, adopting county resolutions and ordinances as authorized by state law, and appointing numerous department heads and boards.

The remaining political authority in the county was divided between leaders who ran for public office and appointees of the governor. Voters elected a Judge of the Circuit Court every 15 years and elected the Circuit Court Clerk, three Orphans' Court Judges, a Register of Wills, a Treasurer, a Sheriff, and a State's Attorney to four-year terms.

Maryland's governor, in consultation with local political party central committees, appointed the District Court Judge, the Board of Education, the Property Tax Assessment Appeal Board, the Board of Supervisors of Elections, the Director of Civil Defense, the Liquor Control Board, and the Board of Trustees of Garrett Community College, who won the battle to establish the college in 1968.

Commissioners needed to stay on the right side of mayors and council members in the county's eight incorporated towns: Accident, Deer Park, Friendsville, Grantsville, Kitzmiller, Loch Lynn Heights, Mountain Lake Park, and the county seat, Oakland.

The commissioners hired managers to run the then county-owned liquor stores ["dispensaries"] in Oakland and Grantsville, and each commissioner hired a constable, a limited authority police officer, for his district.

Other Maryland counties under charter or "code home rule" forms of governance could pass ordinances enabling collective bargaining. But Garrett County's road workers, other county employees and workers paid by the county's incorporated towns could only gain collective bargaining rights if their legislators won them at the General Assembly in Annapolis. Without a countywide ordinance, even if the county's road workers or their peers succeeded in winning union recognition, their contracts would not have the force of law.

The commissioners and the road employees' association had negotiated in relatively good faith despite the lack of legislative fiat. But as two financially conservative commissioners took their seats on the commission and road workers considered affiliating with AFSCME, crews wondered how long the peace would continue.

7

THE COMMUNITY COLLEGE CONTROVERSY

New Commission Elected

"Garrett County's politics is very personal in nature…with so small a total population. A high proportion of the populace is on a first-name basis with their elected officials. If the voter doesn't have first-hand information about the candidate, it's most likely that some member of the voter's widely extended family does. Indeed, a knowledge of genealogy can often be the most useful tool to forecast the results of a local election. Thus, where voters are motivated by longtime personal acquaintance in combination with party loyalty and a 'turn out' tradition, there is minimal need for the panoply of partisan promotional efforts."

    - Tim Dugan, *Western Maryland: A Profile.* [1]

    In November, 1966, John Ross Sines and Hubert Friend were elected to join incumbent Allen S. "Dick" Paugh Sr. on the county commission. All farmers and Republicans, they exemplified the traditional and familial advantages cited by Dugan. Despite their common backgrounds, Friend, Sines and Paugh ended up in persistent, pointed disagreement over how the county should be governed.

John "Ross" Sines

    Ross Sines was elected to the commission after a door-to-door campaign, a challenging exercise in the thinly settled county.
    Sines' forebears were from Germany. His great, great-uncle,

Abraham Lincoln Sines, was the first forest fire chief in Garrett County. Jonas Sines, Ross Sines' father, was an unpaid minister at Pine Grove Church of the Brethren who'd been seriously injured in a coal mine accident. He had served as a county commissioner for 12 years, ending his tenure in 1954.

"I remember grandpap preaching on one leg with the other on a chair [due to his injury in the mines]," said David Sines, Ross Sines' nephew.

Struggling to survive on the family farm, Ross Sines nearly lost his leg when a tractor kicked out of gear and the vehicle rolled over twice. "Dr. Joe Alvarez fixed me up," he said. He remained friends with Alvarez, Oakland's general surgeon, who owned 300 acres nearby and took Sines up in the plane he piloted.

In 1966, Sines was asked by some leading Republicans to run for county commissioner. He faced five other candidates in the primary election and "pulled through with 77 votes" in the general election, defeating the Democrat, James Matthews, half-brother of the popular Rev. Don Matthews, Sines' friend.

"I didn't take money from anybody for my campaign," said Sines, who paid for ads in *The Republican* and "pocket cards." He said, "I just drove through the communities, asking people to vote for me."

"If Matthews [had been elected] with Dick Paugh instead of Sines, it would have been the turning point in recognizing the union," said Andy Lewis, Matthews' son-in-law. "James Matthews was a staunch Democrat and union man," said Lewis, a county road worker who worked as a mechanic in the Oakland and Accident garages, and the son of roads striker Henry Lewis,

The Nov. 3, 1966 issue of *The Republican* ran competing political ads for Matthews and Sines. Sines had shifted his position on building Garrett College, stating that he was "not opposed" to the proposed junior college for Garrett County, but "desired the opportunity" to determine the county's finances and wanted to "listen to the wishes of the people."

Sines promised to keep taxes low and viewed the growing support for Garrett Community College as competing with the real needs of the county. He vowed to improve county services, including roads maintenance.

"I met a woman [back then] whose car got hung up on an (unpaved) road," said Sines. "I asked her if she wanted a college or the road paved."

Matthews strongly favored building the college. He supported the road workers and refuted rumors he had offered to give jobs to some residents and fire others if elected. Matthews had worked as a Teamster at the Mt. Storm power station in nearby West Virginia. He was a member of the Paperworkers Union at Westvaco's paper mill in Luke, and a member of the building trades at S.J. Groves, a road construction company.

Matthews said, "I am in favor of seeing that all county road workers receive fair and equitable pay. This is a time of ever-increasing living conditions that strike the working man hardest and I am in favor of seeing that his income keeps pace with inflation. Nothing less would be fair to him."

On Election Day, Sines won the election by a vote of 2,932 to Matthews' 2,120. Sines won every municipal and rural precinct except Kitzmiller, West Oakland and Avilton.

"We ran on our own. But I appreciated Hubert Friend's experience [in the primary]," said Sines.

Sines said he was supported by many of the county's teachers because he had opposed Willard Hawkins, the county's secretary of education who, he said, was "distrusted" by educators. During the campaign, he accused Hawkins of using county paper to publish campaign material opposing him and Friend.

Sines acknowledged that workers in private industry, like his brother and other relatives, who worked at Bethlehem Steel's plant at Sparrows Point near Baltimore, had the right to form unions. "Workers on the roads had a right to form a union," Sines said. "But, as an elected official, I had a right to refuse to recognize the union."

Hubert Friend

"My dad was really into politics and was very conservative. In the latter days he softened up a little," said Hubert Friend's daughter, Vera Dunithan. "But he just wanted to help the citizens, to do what his dad [a former commissioner] did."

"Dad was busy on the farm, raising dairy cows and Angus cows. He grew potatoes, too, and would take steers to auctions at Friend's Sale Barn. He served on the Garrett County Fair Board," said Dunithan.

She recalled her father using a scythe to cut grass along the fence outside the farm, stopping to sharpen it with a whetstone.

"We went out during lunchtime and picnicked in a field. He would tell my mother [Hazel Brenneman Friend] to pack lunch, and we would go to picnic tables on the farm's lake," said Dunithan.

Hubert Friend was active in the Hoyes Methodist church. Newspapers frequently announced his Bible readings at the church. He "always had to have his cup of coffee, but he didn't drink alcohol or use tobacco," said Ross Sines.

Allen "Dick" Paugh Sr.

"My Dad was a people person," says Carroll Paugh of his father, Allen "Dick" Paugh, first elected to the county commission in 1962.

Carroll Paugh, 83, remembers meeting one of his father's constituents who wanted to buy the property adjacent to a house in Swanton that needed to be torn down. The constituent said he was getting no help from any elected leaders in the county. Exasperated, he talked to Dick Paugh.

The house, said Carroll Paugh, was "torn down and [the property] cleaned up in three days."

Dick Paugh's son said his father invested his work ethic into his farm, his church and community. He was an active member of the Paradise United Methodist Church (formerly United Brethren), where for 30 years he served as treasurer.

Carroll Paugh, who drove a county school bus for more than a half-century, was unable to confirm a much-repeated story that his father had personally mortgaged property to help establish Garrett Community College. Though the tale persists in the county, the college has no record of such an investment.

But Carroll said he wouldn't be surprised if his dad had made such a commitment. "My Dad only had an eighth-grade education," he said, "but he really supported building the college."

Progress and Conflict

As the new commissioners took office in 1966, Garrett County had learned how to compete for federal dollars. President Lyndon Johnson's "War on Poverty" programs (1963-1969) were still delivering significant aid to Appalachia.

Programs covering everything from food assistance to developing local parks and sewerage systems continued during the administration of Richard Nixon, elected in 1969. The State of Maryland supplemented the federal largesse during the terms of Governor Spiro Agnew (1967-1969) and Governor Marvin Mandel (1969-1979).

Attendance at the county's commission meetings blended distinct eras—and points of view—in political life. A still developing bureaucracy left nearly every problem and question for the commissioners to solve.

Commissioner positions were part-time. This, combined with their lack of authority, led to often challenging and tumultuous commission meetings.

Nearly every problem that couldn't be addressed because the commissioners were working their farms during the day was brought to meetings at night. Into the early 1970s, residents would show up at commission meetings carrying the pelts of foxes and coyotes to collect bounties from commissioners for protecting local livestock.

A sign in the commission's offices, still posted at the time of the strike, said: "Effective October 1, it will be necessary to present the whole scalp of any fox, weasel or wildcat in order to receive bounty for same."

Citizens showed up to complain about individual property tax assessments or the rats at the local dump. Residents requested the county's agreed-to cash payment for lambs killed by dogs running loose. There were even complaints about poor fishing on Deep Creek Lake, which was stocked by the state. Commissioners received petitions from communities calling for repair to county roads or the construction of new schools.

Some asked for emergency assistance, like the father asking

for help to send his daughter to an out-of-state hospital. Parents, sometimes in large groups, asked for school renovations or brand-new buildings. Nearly every meeting attracted individual residents and homeowners' associations, many carrying petitions from communities requesting blacktopping of public roads. Developers, too, asked for private roads to be maintained by the county.

Before each fiscal year ended, representatives of the Garrett County Teachers Association usually showed up at the meetings. They were joined by rank-and-file road workers—with or without their association's representatives—and brought grievances over job classifications, benefits, hiring, and discipline. The commissioners heard separately from salaried roads supervisors and school bus contractors wanting more money for their work.

Simultaneously, the social service, business and educational leaders of the county appeared, highlighting their requests for county funds with the latest legislation offering available state and federal grants, loans, and matching funds for impoverished and struggling Appalachian communities.

A state civil defense official asked the commissioners to designate county buildings as nuclear fallout shelters. Brad Rinard from Community Action requested aid for coal mining families being evicted from their homes in Vindex, adjacent to Kitzmiller because of the coal mining downturn.

Chamber of Commerce President Bob Rudy asked the commissioners to hire a full-time planner and to float industrial development bonds. The concept of countywide planning and zoning, one of the sharpest burrs in the county's political thicket, remained unresolved more than five decades later. Citizens were fearful of incurring higher taxes to cover costs for improvements like sidewalks.

The challenges posed by population growth and aging infrastructure, lagging wages, low property values, and slow industrial development left Sines, Paugh, and Friend scrambling to define priorities.

Tim Dugan, a private contractor who worked with the county's planning commission to produce the county's first comprehensive plan in 1973, wrote in *Western Maryland: A Profile:* "It is distressing that 762 families in Garrett (13.8%) had a 1969 income which did not even amount to three-quarters of the poverty level: 17 out of every 100 people in the county lived in severe poverty. One-third of the families in Garrett failed to obtain an income in 1969 that was even 25% above the poverty level." [1]

Facing these challenges and the tight scrutiny of an electorate where county residents say, "Everyone seems to be related to everyone else," the three commissioners' shifted their alliances issue-by-issue, wary of being outshone by each other.

The commissioners were generally aligned on the board's relationship with businesses. They continued the county practice of granting property tax abatements to all firms with more than 20 employees. Before Bausch and Lomb moved from New York to its expansive new sunglasses facility near Oakland, the commission's minutes included cryptic references to infrastructure preparations for a "responsible industrial employer" coming in.

By 1971, the county's bill for building access roads and a sewerage system for Bausch and Lomb, totaled $180,000, a huge investment layered atop the property tax exemption. Under the leadership of economic development director Col. J. Haig Jackson, the county prepared to dam Broadford Run and create a reservoir to help supply water to the plant. Some private land was condemned, generating controversy. In discussions over the damming of Broadford Run, Friend said he was opposed "in principle" to land condemnation.

The three commissioners challenged the environmental lobby on behalf of local extraction industries. They sent a letter to state legislators opposing more stringent regulations on emissions from coal-fired power plants. In his prior term (1962-1966), Paugh joined his fellow commissioners, sending a telegram to the state opposing establishment of the State Water Pollution Commission, fearing it would hurt the profitability of county mines that were discharging wastewater into local streams. In 1963, Paugh supported a coal operator, Carl Harvey, in a pollution dispute with the state.

On many of their decisions, one of the commissioners would refuse to cast a vote or, after making a policy unanimous, release a statement—included in the commission's minutes—explaining his vote to citizens opposed to the measure.

In 1963, Helmuth Heise, the founder of Recreational Industries Inc., which later became the Wisp ski and hotel complex, asked for a $50,000 loan to develop the business. An unnamed source revealed that a member of the county's development commission had not disclosed a financial interest in the project. Paugh refused to join his fellow commissioners supporting the project and voted against the loan.

The federal government largely drove policy for the county's farmers. But in late 1968, the Garrett County Farm Bureau asked the commissioners to eliminate the county's tax on personal farm property and equipment. Sines and Friend displayed political courage opposing the influential bureau, refusing to extend any exemption beyond the current $2,500 per individual farmer.

In a letter to William Umbel, president of the Farm Bureau, Friend wrote: "To decrease further the tax base in the view of rising demands for county expenditures would force the tax rate beyond the point where the average taxpayer could pay, thus affecting your group as seriously as any group in the county." Paugh supported eliminating the personal tax, with the reduction split over two years.

The commissioners shared some socially conservative perspectives. The Rev. Walter Leake, representing the local chapter of the right-wing American Independent Party, showed up at the commission with fellow ministers Homer Mellott and John Justice to oppose the teaching of sex education in the public schools. The three commissioners unanimously signed a letter to the state board of education stating that "talk about sex" should remain the responsibility of parents.

While mostly aligned on business and industry, sometimes the commissioners openly expressed differences in overall philosophy. In March 1968, Sines, a member of the county's Welfare Board, refused to support a motion from Paugh, seconded by Friend, to commit 20 percent of the county's revenues to fund the GCCAC. Sines said the federal community action bureaucracy undermined the resilience and self-reliance of local residents.

In his prior term, Paugh sometimes joined his fellow commissioners, holding a tight line in negotiations with the roads Association. But Paugh continued to maintain close relationships with many of the road workers and their leaders, as well as with members of GCCAC, the board of education, and college trustees. Paugh actively supported a wide range of spending on programs that Sines and Friend said the county could not afford or should be the responsibility of the state or federal government.

Sines cast Paugh's relationships with the GCCAC, the road workers, and professional educators, as well as his support for greater spending, as political opportunism. From the start of his term he made a solemn vow to defeat Paugh in the next commission election.

Despite the commissioners' divergent approaches, the 1966-1970 term was notable for its wide accomplishments, particularly in expanding the county's infrastructure and social safety net.

In May 1966, the commissioners approved a $2,000 appropriation to begin working with the Maryland State Planning Commission on sanitation. In August, a meeting was held with representatives of Baltimore engineering firm Rummel, Klepper and Kahl to discuss a master plan.

In July, 1968, representatives of the Maryland Department of Health met with the county commissioners to discuss financial assistance for water and sewage facilities. Two months later, Bob Rudy and C.C. "Bus" Bender, representing the county's development corporation, suggested the commission hire a qualified planner and appropriate $7,500 to qualify for federal funding for water and sewage development. The commission took no action.

In June 1969, a "redevelopment area" took shape in downtown Oakland as the county invested in the Little Yough Watershed Project for beautification and flood control approved by federal funders.

The county contributed $122,000, the federal government $239,000 to the riverfront modernization that, years later, included a pavilion on the river, site of the town's farmer's market.

The beautification project, however, didn't include stanching the sewage pouring into the river a few hundred feet downriver from the pavilion. The sewage was a longstanding complaint of residents like Julia Rowan, who showed up at a 1967 commission meeting to complain about solid wastes and odors from the polluted river.

There was "still a lot of resentment about environmental rules and regulations," said Edgar Harman, a Cove resident, who was hired by the county's health department in 1963.

"We [health department] used every opportunity to show people the benefits of installing public sewer systems," said Harman. "When the state started putting money into the projects, we would say [the investment] wasn't going to 'break' us and tried to show that the efforts were going to benefit tourism."

Oakland's water treatment needs languished. But in August 1969, the mayors of Loch Lynn and Mountain Lake Park reached agreement on plans for sanitary sewer systems. The Friend commission finally agreed to underwrite a $25,000 loan for the sewage infrastructure development. The commission also moved forward on investments in health and public education.

Commissioners approved an addition to Garrett County Memorial Hospital. Schools were expanded—with state and federal government support—in Accident, Friendsville, Crellin, Kitzmiller, Bloomington and Grantsville. Construction began on a library extension. The runway at the Garrett County Airport (established in 1962) was extended. Discussions began on establishing a county landfill.

Services to the residents living in poverty or facing personal trauma became more professionalized. A food stamp program and improved mental health and substance abuse services were initiated. Community Action launched a youth jobs program that employed 200. A community center was approved for Grantsville.

In June 1969, Sines introduced a motion, seconded by Paugh, to reduce property taxes for residents who had been declared permanently and totally disabled by Social Security and whose yearly gross income didn't exceed $5,000.

Garrett Community College

The sharpest conflicts during the 1966-1970 term centered on education and employment contracts. Disputes over approving and funding Garrett Community College dovetailed with three years of contentious bargaining between the commissioners and the Garrett

County Teachers Association. These bitter confrontations were precursors of the hostility between Paugh and his fellow commissioners over the road workers in 1970.

The prior commission (1962-1966), composed of Paugh, Earl Opel and H.D. (Hub) Swartzentruber, supported the development of Garrett Community College. Many of the county's leaders from both political parties saw the college as essential to attracting new employers and investment. It was a way to keep young people with promising futures from leaving the county.

In June 1966, the college board of trustees informed the commission they planned to purchase farmland from Robert and Maria Glotfelty for its campus. Two months later, the commissioners signed a petition asking the state for a $760,000 grant to begin construction.

Sines and Friend opposed the college trustees plan to purchase the Glotfelty's land, asking the trustees to consider two other tracts.

Paugh continued his advocacy for the college as his second term began. Hubert Friend stated he had made "no commitment" to the college during his campaign. Sines, despite his pivot during his campaign, opposed building the college. Lowell Bender from GCCAC said, "Sines didn't want a college to be built because, he said, it would 'bring in undesirables.'"

Road worker Leo Miller remembered Sines showing up on a jobsite and climbing into Miller's county truck. Banking on Miller's influence as a representative of the Association, Sines asked for Miller's support in opposing county investment in the college.

Said Miller, "I told Sines all you do is oppose spending money. I told him that if the county refused state funds for the college, the money would just be sent to another area."

Attempting to settle the commissioners' dispute over college funding, State Sen. George R. Hughes and Del. B.O. Aiken won an amendment to the Annotated Code of Maryland granting the commissioners of Garrett County the authority to hold a referendum giving the county voters the final say over the establishment of the college.

Referendums enjoyed a long history in the county. Between 1896 and 1968, there were six referendums alone regarding the sale of liquor and beer. In February 1967, Sines moved the county to hold a referendum on Garrett Community College to coincide with a planned June 13 election to decide if Maryland would convene a constitutional convention.

Opposition to the college went beyond Sines and political conservatives. The American Federation of Teachers officially opposed the new school. Teachers' leaders Darrell Malone and Dave Beard and at least one later member of the county's board of education voted no.

"I didn't think the college was necessary," said Beard. "Frostburg State, where I had gone to school, was close. So was West Virginia University. The college took funds away from mandatory education for students in the county's public schools."

Garrett County voters approved establishing the college by a vote of 2,184 to 933. All but three of the county's districts voted with the majority. The same day, the commissioners passed a resolution recognizing the will of the voters. However, when Paugh moved to add $.05 to the county's tax levy to help finance the college, he received no second from Sines or Friend.

In November, between 125 and 150 residents showed up at the county commission meeting in support of the college. Friend and Sines continued to oppose the trustees' choice of the Glotfelty farm site and again refused funds for the college.

The day after the commission meeting, Willard Hawkins, secretary-treasurer of the college's board of trustees, sent a letter to the commissioners saying, "It is indeed a crime and shame that two commissioners can, through their acts of petty political spite work, thwart the will of the people and deny the county this much needed facility.

Hawkins continued, "If the mass protest of your actions staged at the Court House [commission meeting] yesterday told you anything, it was that your day of reckoning will come the first chance the people have to express themselves."

On Dec. 11, Sines and Friend replied, telling Hawkins they were returning his letter because it was "a reflection upon your office and does not belong in our files." The two commissioners wrote: "The undersigned feels the [college] requires serious consideration … and should not be treated in such an undignified manner. We are willing to give consideration to any opinion …In return we ask you to do the same. Furthermore, we are opposed to the expenditure of public money [spent on Hawkins' letter], when the expenditure is designed to influence and sway the public."

Board of Education Sues Commissioners

Two months later, with the college's funding still unresolved, another dispute simmered between Friend and Sines and the Garrett County Board of Education, then still appointed by the governor. The board proposed funding a vocational education campus at Southern High School (Oakland) and building an addition to Northern High School in Accident.

Sines and Friend refused to sign the vocational school grant, asking Hawkins to appear before the board.

Hawkins, appointed superintendent in 1954, was a native of Sykesville, Maryland, the son of a general store owner. He had graduated from Western Maryland College, then received a law degree from Lasalle Extension School. He completed other course work at the University of Virginia and Johns Hopkins University.

He served as president of the Carroll and Dorchester County Teachers Associations and, later, as president of the Maryland Secondary Principals Association. "My father was passionate about education. He was strong-willed, intellectual and articulate," said Willard "Bill" Hawkins Jr.

His father, he said, maintained good relationships with Mennonite and Amish families, working closely with Esther Yoder, the principal of the Yoder School outside Grantsville that primarily served members of the two religious communities, but received financial support from the public school budget.

But, said the younger Hawkins, his father had run into controversy as he consolidated some of the other elementary schools. "He was faced with baseball bats [carried by parents] when he tried to consolidate a one-room schoolhouse in Finzel."

Hawkins had a history of taking disputes with the commissioners directly to parents of school-age children. In 1965, he testified before the U.S. House Subcommittee on Education and Labor, bringing a newsletter he'd sent to county parents excoriating county commissioners who were not making use of state and federal funds to improve teacher salaries and school facilities.

The three-member Garrett County Board of Education approved Hawkins' testimony before Congress. Ms. Jackie Brady, a Kitzmiller schoolteacher, and Clinton Englander, an Oakland pharmacist, were both prominent Democrats, appointed by Democratic Governor J. Millard Tawes. Republican George D. Edwards, a Grantsville car dealer, was the grandfather of Republican State Senator George Edwards.

Englander served on the Oakland City Council and as president of the Maryland State PTA. He helped establish WMSG, (AM, later FM) radio station in Oakland and was an original investor in Marsh Mountain, now WISP resort. An accomplished painter, classical guitarist, skier and SCUBA diver, he served on the vestry of St. Matthews Episcopal Church and on the Southern Garrett Rescue Squad.

"My daddy was all about everyone having a good education, based upon how hard he had to work to get his own," said Englander's daughter, Barbara Englander. Her father, born in 1918, grew up in working-class Michigan and earned a degree in pharmacy from Wayne State University before entering the Marine Corps in WWII as an aviation cadet. He attained the rank of Lt. Commander as a Sonar officer in the Pacific Theater.

Moving to Oakland after the war, Englander established the pharmacy in a building that still bears his name decades after the business closed.

"Before Garrett Community College was built, people around here mostly didn't go to college unless they went to Potomac State in West Virginia or Frostburg," said Englander, who lived on her father's former Christmas tree farm, adjacent to property owned by a relative of Ross Sines.

Despite his differences with Sines, Englander said her father maintained a respectful relationship with the outspoken Republican farmer who shopped in his store. Sines, she said, came by to offer condolences after her father died in 2012.

Jackie Burrell Brady, the first woman to serve on the board of education, was a graduate of Piedmont College in Demorest, Georgia. Her father, Fitzhugh Burrell, had moved to Maryland from the mountains of northern Georgia prior to World War II. He and his brothers opened a coal mine, hand-loading coal into cars pulled by ponies.

The Burrell Brothers operation was all union and Jackie Brady was, said her son, Mike, all Democrat, "a feisty woman who wasn't afraid to say what was on her mind."

Brady began her teaching career as a Head Start instructor, then taught elementary school for 22 years at Oak Creek School and Broadford and Kitzmiller Elementary Schools. She served on the county's health planning council and on the boards of the Ruth Enlow Library and the county's social services. To honor her town's history, Brady founded and curated the Kitzmiller Coal Heritage Museum.

George D. Edwards began his working life in a sawmill in Crellin, just outside of Oakland. He moved to Grantsville and established the George D. Edwards and Sons Grantsville Garage. It included a new car dealership.

"Grandpa treated his customers with dignity just as he did our students as a member of the Garrett County Board of Education for many years," said former State Senator George Edwards. "He was an honest, hard-working, dedicated man who would give you the shirt off his back to help you out."

Looking back, Sines said he and Friend were denying money to the schools, in part, to help push Englander, Brady and Edwards to fire Hawkins.

"A blue-ribbon committee [later] came in from Montgomery County and rounded up the commissioners to be interviewed about Hawkins. The school board got rid of him," said Sines.

In 1968, Hawkins, still serving on the general council of the Maryland State Teachers Association, resigned as superintendent. Raymond O. McCullough, a native of Friendsville, who had served as principal of two Allegany County high schools and as an assistant superintendent in Howard County, replaced Hawkins.

The Garrett County Board of Education, joined by the Trustees of Garrett Community College, filed a writ with the Circuit Court demanding the commissioners reply to the board on the high school and college funding. On January 15, Sines and Friend were served with a summons to appear in court for their refusal to support the grants.

Judge Stuart B. Hamill ruled for the boards. With Friends' and Sines' opposition derailed, the college was established on Sept. 13, 1969 and the Glotfelty tract became the site of the school.

Today, located adjacent to a campus building, Allen S. Paugh Sr. Rd. honors the commissioner who championed its establishment.

Shelby Glotfelty Paugh, later the wife of Dick Paugh's nephew, was hired by the Garrett County Health Department in 1955. She'd just graduated from Northern High School. Mrs. Paugh said Sines' opposition to spending money on the college was mirrored by his opposition to spending on public health.

"I used to visit Sines' office with the county's chief public health officer," said Paugh. "He would always dig in his [desk] drawers and not pay attention whenever the health officer asked for funding."

Fifty-two years later, when asked about the school, now called Garrett College, Sines said he still believed that "higher education has ruined America."

[1] Thomas H. Hattery, *Western Maryland: A Profile (Lomond Publications, 1980). p. 17.*

8

THE UNIONS STAND UP

Garrett County Teachers Association Contract

In June, 1966, members and leaders of the Garrett County Teachers Association (GCTA) showed up at the county commission, requesting $400 across-the-board wage increases (covering all members of the union).

The teachers cautioned that Garrett County would have a hard time filling the large number of imminent retirements, with teacher paychecks inferior to those in neighboring Allegany County. The commissioners took no action. Two weeks later the teachers returned with the same request. Again, no action.

The county teachers were accustomed to benign neglect at best. Martha DeBerry, who served as secretary of the teachers' association, taught math at Southern High School before she was moved by administrators to the school's library to replace a retiring librarian. When DeBerry, later a board member of the county's historical society, questioned administrators why a newly hired male teacher had taken her math position, she was told, "We can't have a man working as a librarian."

In May, 1967, Commissioner Dick Paugh moved for approval of the teachers' request for $400 across-the-board increases. He received no second. Sines and Friend requested an audit of teachers' salaries. They passed a motion mandating that all mail received by the commission from residents on the teachers' request for a raise be "kept secret" from the public. Paugh did not vote on either measure.

In January, 1968, teacher representatives Foster Riggs, Carl Everly and Lawrence Myers returned to the county commission asking for raises totaling $280,000, requesting the commissioners respond by March 19. Sines told the teachers no increase should be granted by the county unless the State of Maryland helped fund the measure.

In March, Sines moved that teachers' salaries be increased by a grand total of $175,000. He provided a listing of how the increases should be spread among job classifications. He stated the county's income tax surcharge would need to be increased from the minimum of 20 percent to approximately 50 percent to fund the increases. But, he said, that measure would still leave inadequate funds that would have to come from other sources of revenue. Friend seconded Sines' motion. Paugh did not vote. The teachers rejected the county's offer.

Garrett County Board of Education members George Edwards, Clinton Englander and a new member, Diane Thayer, appeared before the commissioners in late February requesting a settlement of the dispute to "ward off a strike" by teachers. At the commission meeting, GCTA leaders vehemently refuted talk of a strike, telling the commissioners, "Statements [about a strike] to be taken by teachers were not the official action of the GCTA board."

Recalling the dispute, Walter Johnson, who was part of the teachers' association delegation, said, "The association worked closely with the board of education. We knew they were limited in funds. We understood that. And the teachers would never have gone on strike."

Paugh, Sines and Friend continued to argue over teacher pay increases, with teachers voting down another counteroffer from Sines and Friend. Presaging the polarization over the roads strike, the legislative committee of the Garrett County Farm Bureau brought two motions to a commission meeting regarding teacher pay.

First, they urged the commissioners to continue negotiating with the teachers' association. Then, they read from the text of a Farm Bureau letter to GCTA president, Lawrence Myers stating, "We deplore the idea of having the teachers break their contract in a 'strike.' In the case of a strike, any support from the Farm Bureau shall be discontinued."

The warning was extreme considering the teachers' association's leadership disavowing any plan to strike. In May 1969, the board of commissioners finally approved pay increases amounting to 7% of the teachers' payroll.

"Garrett County has always been low on the pole for teacher pay and probably always will be," said Walter Johnson, who began teaching at Southern High School in 1968 and was later elected leader of the GCTA. The son of an Oakland dry cleaner shop owner and one of 11 children, Johnson graduated high school with Ross Sines.

Attesting to Sines' stubbornness, Johnson said, "You can't be so tight-fisted that you can't advance and make some real progress and begin to grow." Sines, he said, was elected by farmers who "didn't want all this growth."

Labor Disputes Divide Commission

With no public unions in the county outside of the teachers, nearly all other grievances and pay disputes — including those of the road employees' association — came directly before the commissioners. During the 1966-1970 term, employees asking for more money included school bus contractors, roads department supervisors, sheriffs and nearly all county employees.

Until the roads strike revealed the county's failings in modern "human resource management," hiring for all county jobs was done directly by the commissioners. At nearly every meeting, residents would show up looking for jobs, including sons asking to replace their fathers who had retired from jobs on the roads.

In April 1966, the commissioners approved the establishment of a youth corps that would employ students to work up to 28 hours per week for $1.25 an hour, paid for with federal grants. The board advised Robert Stemple, the county's welfare director, to take as many youths into the program as possible to assist on the county roads.

The same month, Roads Department Chief Engineer Paul DeWitt appeared before the commission accompanied by an outside consultant to discuss a study on the feasibility of establishing a merit system covering county employees.

DeWitt said such a system would encourage "good" employees to stay, rather than leave county employment. The contractor requested $1,000 to begin the study. No decision was made on whether to hire

92

the contractor or even to consider a merit system.

Direct hiring and firing of road workers by the commissioners would soon become even more contentious as Sines and Friend fired DeWitt. But another firing would come first.

Court Clerk Fired

Immediately after being sworn into office on Dec. 7, 1966, Sines and Friend moved to fire the commission's clerk, Virginia Fizer. Paugh objected to Fizer's firing, contending that Fizer had done a good job. He also suggested the commissioners contact Del. B.O. Aiken and State Senator George Hughes to introduce a bill in Annapolis establishing a merit system in the county. Friend responded, "We won't take any hiring away from the commissioners." Sines said, "The faces should be changed before changing policy [establishing a merit system]."

Fizer requested a discussion over the reasons for her discharge. Sines and Friend expressed no dissatisfaction with Fizer's work. She was skilled in shorthand and kept meticulous minutes. But Sines accused Fizer of spreading information about internal commission affairs outside the office so frequently that some folks told him, "Virginia is running the county."

The commissions' minutes, prepared by Fizer, stated: "Mrs. Fizer advised Mr. Sines that she had never tried to run the county, but that when people came to the office for information that she was able to furnish … she did not believe it was necessary to bother the commissioners at their homes." When Sines asked Fizer [in the same meeting] if she had anyone to suggest filling her position, she told the commissioners they "probably would not find anyone" to work for her low pay. She refused to train her replacement and demanded her accrued vacation pay.

Fifty years later, recalling Fizer's termination, Sines said, "She lasted only three weeks. I fired her after she came over to my desk wearing a low-cut dress. I told Hubert [Friend], "We need to get rid of her." Fizer's firing only amplified an ongoing dispute over the commissioners' hiring and firing procedures.

But all discussion of establishing a merit system stayed off the table until 1968, when Sines moved that Joseph Welch and former State Senator Clifford Friend be appointed to serve as members of a commission to study establishing a merit system. Hubert Friend seconded the motion. Paugh did not vote. Two years later, Clifford Friend became the most outspoken county resident opposing union recognition for county road workers, frequently writing inflammatory letters published in *The Republican*. In one letter, he called AFSCME organizers "strong armed goons sent to threaten and intimidate public officials. "

Sines: "Association is Not Running The Roads"

On December 19, Earl Sebold, who retired from the county roads department, told the commissioners he had left due to illness, but now wanted to return. He said his Grantsville Garage co-workers, members of the Association, had voted 100 percent for his reinstatement. Sines and Friend were sympathetic to Sebold's request.

But Sines issued a challenge. "The association should be informed," said Sines, "that they were not running the roads department, that the management was up to the commissioners." Sines' attitude toward the road workers earned a nickname that would survive through the road strike and into his retirement: "Hard Times Sines."

After firing Fizer, Sines moved to discharge Roads Department Chief Engineer Paul DeWitt. DeWitt should be replaced "for the betterment of the county," said Sines, claiming he had heard many complaints during his campaign about DeWitt's management and how he was "allowing his relatives on Sang Run (once called 'DeWitttown' for the family's predominance in the area) to 'run things on the roads.'"

Sines said, "It was a hard decision [to fire DeWitt] because Paul was a friend and a member of my church." Paugh opposed DeWitt's firing. Sines and Friend sent a letter to DeWitt advising him they were looking for his replacement. Paugh refused to sign the termination letter, then introduced a motion providing that a licensed engineer replace DeWitt. The motion died for lack of a second.

"How Shall Two Walk Together Except They Be Agreed?"

The next day, DeWitt presented a letter of resignation. Outlining his differences with Sines and Friend, he quoted Amos 3:3: "How shall two walk together except they be agreed?" DeWitt rejected the charge of nepotism, telling the commissioners he had turned down a relative who had persistently pushed to be hired.

The minutes cite Paugh: "He felt Mr. DeWitt had done a good job that the roads were better, working conditions better and better machinery was available to do the work with."

The minutes continued: "Mr. Sines stated that Mr. DeWitt had made enemies over the county and there was dissatisfaction among the men." Sines said he "did not know if all the opposition was just" and that he had considered recommending the hiring of a professional employee [for roads supervisor] and moving Mr. DeWitt from the Roads office to the County Commissioner's Office as a clerk. "But it seemed all were 'down on Dewitt.'" Friend stated, "There should be a 'better understanding' between the commissioners, engineer and foremen."

Paugh asked DeWitt for a suggestion for his replacement. DeWitt recommended supervisor Clayton Smith as a temporary fill-in. After DeWitt left his keys with the commissioners, Paugh reintroduced his motion providing for a licensed engineer to replace DeWitt. The motion passed unanimously.

Freshly appointed, Clayton Smith questioned the commissioners about the upcoming annual roads department Christmas Party. Sines advised that alcohol should be prohibited. Friend agreed but stipulated there should be "no penalties" issued to workers for drinking. The commissioners voted to give each road worker a five-dollar cash gift.

Decades later, circumstances surrounding DeWitt's firing were still disputed between Sines and DeWitt's family. Sines said DeWitt had shown up at Sines' farm before his election and promised he would help Sines get elected. So, Sines and Friend left DeWitt in his position until after the election. Sines claimed that, after the election, he was still troubled by DeWitt's alleged nepotism and said DeWitt quit only because he "saw the handwriting on the wall and was tipped off by Dick Paugh [about his firing]."

Debra DeWitt, Paul DeWitt's daughter, a retired Garrett County schoolteacher, said her father's resignation letter criticized Sines, to whom she was related on her mother's side, for believing "people should live off nothing and failing to understand that everyone doesn't farm for a living [having to pay for the food that farmers grow]."

Three days after DeWitt's firing, Paugh moved the commissioners approve a seven- percent raise for county road workers, effective July 1. The commissioners had already approved fringe benefit increases. Friend seconded Paugh's motion. Sines voted no on the pay increase, stating that road workers had received a 10 percent increase the previous July, contending "this [latest] increase is putting County employees above average employee wages of our County at this time."

One month later, the commissioners entertained a proposal that vacation and sick leave for all county employees outside of the roads department be made uniform. In June 1967, Sines moved to freeze the wages of all county salaried employees. Friend seconded the motion. Roads department supervisors immediately challenged the wage freeze.

Supervisors Ronald Steyer, Stanley Savage, Stanley Wood, George DeWitt, Herb McCrobie, James Fike and Jonas Peck told the commissioners there was "too little spread" between supervisors and hourly workers, requesting the same percentage increase as the association's members. They also asked for a second supervisor to be assigned the night shift, requested their sick leave to be increased from 18 to 30 days and asked to be paid for overtime hours worked.

1968 Roads Agreement

In June, 1968, the county road workers' association signed a two-year agreement with the county commissioners. The agreement included rates of pay: labor rate $1.97/hour; light operators $2.10/hour; chauffeurs $2.37/hour; operators $2.44/hour; shop foremen $2.50/hour. The contract provided 13 holidays, hospital insurance and 30 days of sick leave. After the agreement was signed, the county hired a new engineer to lead the roads department — Tom Sluss, a Frostburg resident.

It's unlikely Sines and Friend knew where Sluss stood on the question of union recognition. "Tom Sluss was a nice guy who was for the union," said one of the road workers, an early union supporter. "He told us, 'You can have one of the best unions [AFSCME] there ever was if you stay with it.'"

In August, having gone a year with no response on their requests for more money, sick leave and manpower, roads foremen not covered by the Association's contract returned to the commission, accompanied by their new engineer, Tom Sluss. Present in the meeting were supervisors Jonas Peck, Ron Steyer, John Filsinger, Bernard Nally, James Fike, Stanley Wood, John Tasker, Foster Martin, Lyden Holler, and George DeWitt.

Paugh moved that foremen be paid for all hours over 40 at the current hourly rate, leaving all other requests unanswered. The motion passed unanimously. The commissioners' small concession didn't placate the supervisors. Two years later, nearly all the foremen in the meeting joined their co-workers on the picket lines.

But only fifteen months after his hiring, Sluss was gone. The September 1969 commission minutes included a letter of resignation from Sluss, who complained of "working conditions becoming progressively unbearable with each passing day." He added, "I hesitate to elaborate on this matter so as not to be misconstrued, and so that no unbiased insinuations can be made against the many fine friends I have made since my short stay in the county."

On September 9, The *Sun* tied Sluss's resignation to frustration with the county's politics, where individual commissioners "overruled the orders of the chief engineer and sent workers to build and repair roads providing access to the farms of friends." The paper quoted Sluss: "It's impossible to maintain roads this way."

Real estate agent Tom Bernard says, "That boy, Tom Sluss, was the best thing that ever happened to the county. He had been a state roads inspector. He convinced commissioners to phase out tar and chipping and was able to show them blacktopping was an investment."

Sluss's recommendation for roads crews to "stay with AFSCME" was vindicated. One month after his resignation, 120 men among the 144 members of the Garrett County Road Employees' Association signed cards authorizing a merger of the association into AFSCME.

Woody Guthrie said a human being is "a great big hoping machine." In a wide but tight-knit county, the road workers' "hoping machines" were busy. They were even starting to pull along individual entrepreneurs, including school bus drivers, encouraging them to find a collective voice, too.

School Bus Owners Join the Campaign

Approximately 80 school bus owners, who dispatched 112 vehicles, providing all transportation services to the county schools, had always bargained for their services separately. In early April 1968, the bus owners showed up at the commission together asking for a 15-percent increase in pay. They returned two weeks later, represented by fellow owner and Grantsville Democrat Charles "Bus" Bender, asking for a decision.

Dick Paugh moved that the contractors be awarded $30,000 in total increases, providing the State of Maryland contribute $15,000. His motion died for lack of a second. However, Hubert Friend said he would support the motion upon notification the state had decided to split the difference.

The contractors returned to the commission twice more in April. On their last visit, they came before the board as the School Bus Owners Association. They agreed to reduce their increase request to 10 percent. Paugh moved that the commission approve a $21,000 raise for bus contractors, with one-half the sum paid by the county's board of education. Friend seconded the motion. Sines opposed the motion, stating he would vote for no increases until the state, not the county board of education, contributed.

One year later, the bus drivers' association had still received no increase. They returned to the commission represented by Roger Bond, Kyle Bennett, Ira Yates, Richard Thomas, Asa Nethken, Robert Harvey and Playford Ryan. The commissioners approved a letter to be sent to the state requesting help paying the contractors. Once again Friend and Paugh approved a motion to grant $21,000 in additional compensation, with the board of education sharing the cost.

Sines refused to support the increase, continuing his uncompromising fiscal conservatism. But "Hard Times Sines" was also creating yet another influential group of adversaries. Like the road workers, the bus drivers' influence reached into every community.

One year later, the driver-owners would repudiate Sines' hard line with AFSCME Local 1834. As vocal as the students on their buses, the driver-owners complained about potential damage to their buses from unmaintained roads as the road workers strike dragged on.

On July 29, 1970, amid the conflict, the drivers increased the road strikers' leverage, defiantly vowing to refuse to work if the roads weren't repaired by the start of the next school year. Restlessness with the county commission's stance on pay and benefits even spread to the men charged with keeping the public order.

Sheriffs Request Pay Increases

On Sept. 2, 1968, Sheriff James Frantz appeared before the county commission accompanied by Deputy Sheriffs John Evans and Delbert Swartzentruber, requesting a salary increase for deputies and an improved expense account for Frantz.

Paugh moved that deputy sheriffs' salaries be raised to $4,500 per year and Frantz be paid $25 per month until "transportation is provided." His motion died for lack of a second.

A week later, Frantz, who lived adjacent to the jail, returned to the commission. He reported that prisoners in the county jail had not received their breakfast because Mrs. Frantz, his wife, had quit her job as the jail's cook. He told the commissioners his wife had been cooking for prisoners for several years and should be awarded a salary increase and "other considerations."

The commissioners reminded Frantz that he received $1.25 per day to cover board for each prisoner, and $100 per month for a cook. They told him to work out how to use the funds in the "best possible way."

Commissioners were facing a swell of demands, covering a wide range of responsibilities. With their local focus and geographic isolation, they were ill prepared for the upcoming battle—a union challenge greater than the Commissioners had ever faced before.

9

FROM POTHOLES TO POTSHOTS

AFSCME Roads Organizing Peaks

By 1959, 70 percent of AFSCME's members nationwide were blue-collar workers. [1] The union's organizers in Maryland had roots in the industrial sector and the military. They included Will Stoll and Lou Mellick. Stoll, a German-American machinist at the B&O Railroad, was a Marine Corps WWII veteran. Mellick, a union bricklayer, was assigned to Anne Arundel and Harford County.

Tom Kelleher, who joined AFSCME as a staff representative in 1974, recalled joining a "tough" group of elder staff members, citing Stoll's prowess.

"Will Stoll made landings in the South Pacific and was a Marine Corps boxer. He had big hands, but was soft spoken," said Kelleher, who previously worked for the Maryland Classified Employees Association. He had been hired by the MCEA after his return from Navy service in Vietnam and graduation with a degree in sociology from Towson State University.

Kelleher described John Clark, the president of Baltimore City Workers Local 44, as a 300-pound former Army boxer. Clark and fellow city workers and AFSCME reps, Randy Fitzgerald, Howard Johnson and Val Wilson, all weighed between 250 and 300 pounds and were known as "Tons of Fun."

Kelleher recalled Wilson as a "nice man who didn't take any crap." Wilson, said Kelleher, came to his aid during a tough organizing campaign where AFSCME was competing with the Laborers and the Teamsters.

The Glenn L. Martin aviation factory in the Baltimore County town of Middle River provided a rich source of AFSCME talent and leadership at the union's local, state, and national levels.

Ernie Crofoot, Ed Mohler, former coal miner Tom Rapanotti, and legendary organizer Panfilo "P.J." Ciampa—a key leader in the Memphis sanitation strike—all worked in the plant that employed more than 52,000 workers during WWII. They were members of the United Auto Workers, which represented all production workers in the plant.

Ernie "Butch" Crofoot Jr. said his father, who later helped negotiate AFSCME's first roads agreement with the Garrett County commissioners, grew up on Maryland's Eastern Shore, the son of German immigrants.

Crofoot spoke fluent German and attended high school at Archmere Academy, a Catholic prep school in nearby Delaware, his tuition paid by a friend's physician father. Crofoot tried to enlist in military service, hoping to put his German language skills to work, but was rejected three times due to a childhood case of tuberculosis. After getting a job at Glenn L. Martin, he was quickly assigned as a UAW shop steward.

Crofoot joined AFSCME soon after he lost a UAW election. He had a "relatively fast ride" to higher offices in his new union, said his son, later becoming an International Vice President of AFSCME, simultaneously leading the union's powerful Council 67 based in Baltimore.

The former UAW members were the nucleus of AFSCME's widely publicized efforts between 1968 and 1969 to organize Baltimore City's sanitation workers and nearby Harford County's road workers .

Baltimore was engulfed in the uprising that came in the wake of Dr. Martin Luther King's 1968 assassination, with 5,800 arrests, six deaths and an estimated $12 million of damage to property.

P.J. Ciampa had won notoriety in the Memphis sanitation strike, during which Dr. King was murdered. He marched with King and was pictured in newspapers lying in the street as police sprayed strikers with chemical crowd-control agents.

After the Baltimore uprising, Ciampa marshaled AFSCME's efforts to organize Baltimore's sanitation workers. AFSCME competed to win exclusive bargaining rights against the Laborer's union and the MCEA, which represented an estimated 477 of the city's 1,200 sanitation department employees.

Claiming majority status, AFSCME authorized its first strike in the State of Maryland on September 8, 1968, seeking a 25-percent increase in pay. Ciampa faced off with newly elected Baltimore mayor Thomas D'Alesandro III, "Young Tommy," the son of a mayor and the brother of future House of Representatives Speaker Nancy Pelosi.

D'Alesandro immediately secured an injunction against AFSCME. He told the *Baltimore Sun* he sought to gain the "practical advantage of ending the picket lines and the "psychological advantage" of labeling the strikers as lawbreakers.

"Champ" Ciampa challenged "Young Tommy." And he won the last word in *The Sun*, warning the paper's readership the mayor's "psychological" weapon was bound to fail because the men [sanitation workers] were "determined that the only thing that's going to pick up that garbage is more cents per hour."

"[D'Alesandro] is playing the game most mayors play," said Ciampa, comparing Baltimore's new mayor to Henry Loeb, the mayor of Memphis during the sanitation strike. "For 25 cents an hour, health insurance and fringe benefits, he [D'Alesandro] can stop the strike."

The strike was settled on September 11, 1968 with the union ratifying $2.7 million in wage and benefit increases and AFSCME Local 44 securing its majority status among the city's sanitation crews.

Garrett County to Baltimore County

Severe unemployment and low wages had pushed some residents of Garrett County to seek industrial jobs in Baltimore long before AFSCME organizers made their way to the mountains. Middle River and neighboring Eastern Baltimore County communities, Essex, and Dundalk, had already developed strong connections to Garrett County.

Ross Sines' brother was one of dozens of Garrett County workers, including the relatives of many roads' workers, who were hired at Bethlehem Steel's mill, shops, and shipyard at Sparrows Point.

103

Mabel Butler, the wife of roads worker Berman Butler, and Jim Fike, the former roads foreman, both had sisters in Dundalk. Mary Frazee, the wife of roads worker Floyd Frazee, had family members at Bethlehem Steel working alongside the brother of Garrett County entrepreneur Ray Mattingly, owner of Manor Home Center, a lawn and farm equipment store in Mountain Lake Park. Asa Wilhelm's son-in-law worked at Eastern Stainless Steel in Baltimore County. His daughter worked nearby at Glen L. Martin.

Many migrating Garrett County residents never truly left the county behind. Albert "Junior" Shaffer, a Kitzmiller native, for instance, lived in a trailer at Williams Estates, a quarter mile up the road from the Glenn L. Martin plant, while he was employed by Bethlehem Steel. For 30 years, he kept his home in Garrett County, frequently making the long trip back to the mountains.

Kitzmiller native James Lyons, whose mother, Cathy, became the president of AFSCME Local 1834 after the strike, remembers his father, Clarence Lyons, and several other residents crowding into the back of a dump truck and heading to Baltimore for work.

Harford County Road workers Organize

The victory in Baltimore energized AFSCME's efforts in the state. By April 1969, the union had signed contracts in Baltimore, Cumberland, Hagerstown, Montgomery County, and Rockville. AFSCME set up 34 local offices, winning dues check-off and grievance procedures.

Ciampa, Crofoot, Stoll and Mellick next targeted Harford County, 22 miles northeast of Baltimore, population 115,000, home since 1917 to the U.S. Army's Aberdeen Proving Ground.

Annual paychecks of road workers in the mostly rural county, covering 527 square miles at the top of the Chesapeake Bay were only $600 above the state's poverty level. And road crew pay and benefits lagged severely behind neighboring Baltimore County, where workers had organized with AFSCME.

Sometime in 1969, salaried workers formed the Harford County Employees Association, affiliated with the MCEA. AFSCME moved to block any interest in the MCEA among the county's highway workers, who constituted around 100 of the county's 325 employees.

In February 1969, Crofoot asked the county to authorize dues check-off for approximately 80 county highway department workers who had signed AFSCME authorization cards. The county took 10 days to reply to Crofoot. Howlett Cobourn, the commission's president, said he would not grant dues check-off because it would imply recognition of AFSCME. He told the *Sun* that his "inclination" was to "go along" with the Harford County Employees Association. And he said he wouldn't talk to AFSCME until the county's civil service board "knew the outcome" of a discussion in Annapolis concerning collective bargaining.

On April 21, Harford County Road workers struck for union recognition. Fifteen days into the strike, AFSCME's Crofoot, Stoll, Mellick and Clyde Thompson accompanied dozens of county road workers to a meeting of the Harford County Council to again ask for union recognition and the right to collective bargaining.

The commission refused the request. Union representatives and highway workers refused to leave the council chamber. They sat in, played cards and checkers and ignored orders to leave, reported the *Sun*. Thirty-two sit-in participants were arrested for trespassing, including Crofoot, Mellick, Stoll and Thompson. The arrests garnered headlines and photos in local newspapers.

Two weeks into the strike, two Harford County state legislators, both Democrats, proposed a three-step plan for resolving the strike. They endorsed making the county's wage scale for highway workers competitive with counties of similar size. They proposed that workers who did not return to work on the date mandated by the county be fired. And they proposed that the county's landfills, closed since the start of the strike, be reopened with police protection, if necessary, for trucks to get through picket lines.

With primary elections underway, AFSCME set up picket lines at polling places to protest any opening of the landfills.

The strike was settled on May 12, with the county granting voluntary dues deductions and the drafting of grievance procedures. The Harford County victory, staged in a rural county that had turned decidedly Republican since WWII, now shifted AFSCME's attention to Garrett County and Allegany County's Cumberland.

In the mid 1960s, AFSCME's Ed Mohler, a former Glenn L. Martin worker who later became head of the Maryland AFL-CIO, hired Michael Lindner to organize in Western Maryland and neighboring Pennsylvania. Linder had previously worked as an assistant engineer with C&P Telephone Co. [now Verizon], serving as president of Cumberland-based Local 2109 of the Communications Workers of America.

The son of a renowned Allegany County beekeeper, Linder had been active in local politics, running for public office and helping direct AFL-CIOs COPE (Committee on Political Education) efforts in Western Maryland. He actively opposed the 1964 candidacy of George Wallace, the former segregationist governor of Alabama.

"It is most imperative that we repudiate the carpetbagger from Alabama," Lindner told the *Cumberland News*. "The hate and prejudice Governor Wallace advocates has the power to ruin our country."

In 1966, after being hired by AFSCME, Linder ran an unsuccessful campaign for Maryland State delegate. But he also began successful efforts to organize public workers in Chambersburg, Pennsylvania, 88 miles northeast of Cumberland, making that borough's workforce only the second in the state to organize. York County was first.

"We had no experience in organizing and Mike Lindner helped us," said Jim Umbrell, who worked in one of Chambersburg's warehouses for $1.37 per hour with no retirement or medical benefits and no vacation time. In 1969, one year after Lindner and Umbrell won AFSCME's campaign for recognition, workers briefly walked off the job. The job action gave Lindner the leverage to negotiate a first agreement, winning higher pay, shift differentials, increased sick leave and a grievance and arbitration procedure.

"I remember my father making weekly trips to Chambersburg," said Billy Lindner, Michael's oldest son. "And he was always helping with local union picnics around Cumberland, borrowing my grandfather's [the beekeeper's] big-bodied truck to carry beer and food."

Lindner couldn't replicate the Chambersburg success in his hometown. In 1969, he joined AFSCME's campaign to organize non-professional employees at Cumberland Memorial Hospital. The hospital agreed to hold a union certification election. AFSCME lost by more than 2-to-1 in a 250 to 114 vote.

The inspirational victory in Chambersburg and the defeat in Cumberland reinforced the necessity for AFSCME to win a victory in Garrett County. The job was assigned to Michael Lindner.

Soon he was getting help from men like Ray Metz, the son of a union coal miner from Lonaconing in Allegany County. Before being hired as a supply officer for the State Highway Administration in 1958, Metz worked for his father. The elder Metz, a United Mine Workers member, opened his own big vein mine, but continued to pay dues to the union, later retiring on a union pension and black lung benefits.

At the state highway department outside of Cumberland in LaVale, Metz joined the Maryland Classified Employees Association (MCEA) and was elected president of the association's Chapter 4.

"I soon found out," said Metz, "[that] MCEA was not a union. Every employee could belong, and supervisors and bosses dominated the association." We called the MCEA the "Management Controlled Employee Association," he said. "There was no grievance procedure, and all the rules and regulations were made by management with no input from the employees."

"I tried to help the members with their grievances to no avail," he added.

In 1959, Metz left the MCEA and helped bring a section of LaVale's state highway workers into AFSCME. Local 669 was the union's first highway local in the state and Metz served as its president. A couple years after organizing the LaVale local, Metz traveled to Garrett County to help Lindner organize state highway workers there.

Garret County

"Garrett County was very Republican and very anti-union," said Metz, who set up organizing meetings at a local bank, paying for use

107

Standing with Local 1834 President Jack Sowers, AFSCME International President Jerry Wurf (left) said the county commissioners were "depending on hunger and privation to prevent the men from making their own choices...This is not the American way of doing things."

Calvin "Leo" Rinker (third from left), a wounded veteran of the Battle of the Bulge, was elected president of AFSCME Local 1834 after the strike.

Commissioner Ross Sines (arms folded) and Rev. Homer Mellott, circulated Bible tracts during the confrontation over the bus rented to carry strikebreakers through the picket lines.

AFSCME members and officers from Garrett County and Baltimore were excited after driving the strikebreakers from the bus on the town parking lot on August 4, 1970.

Jim and Helen Fike. Photo taken by Len Shindel.

Allen "Dick" Paugh, Garrett County commissioner, who endorsed union recognition. Photo courtesy of Allen's son, Carroll Paugh.

AFSCME's collage of the strike hangs in the county's Oakland garage and the union's office in Baltimore.

Local 1834 President Jack Sowers displays $5,000 check from AFSCME international union to help sustain the strikers.

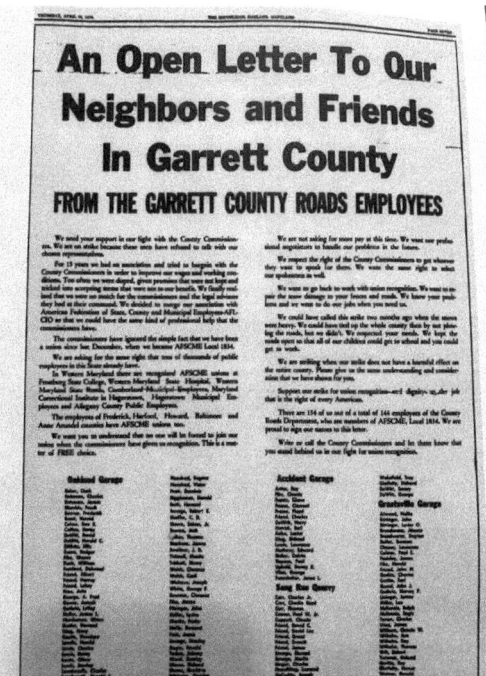

AFSCME Local 1834 made its case to the community in an open letter to The Republican, saying the timing of the strike was planned not to interfere with snow removal enabling the safety of school buses and motorists.

of a room. "The bank would take our money and none of the workers would show up," he said, adding that he brought several workers up from the LaVale shop to knock on doors of highway workers [to talk about joining AFSCME]. Those doors, he recalled, "would slam on us."

In time, Metz developed strong relationships with a few of the highway workers, including Bennie Beckman, Ray Coddington and James Spear, who later was elected mayor of Friendsville.

"The guys we signed up [for AFSCME] were very loyal," said Metz. But even after the group was recruited, Metz faced worker opposition in Garrett County he hadn't experienced in adjoining Allegany and Washington Counties.

Metz filed a grievance because the state wasn't supplying ice to chill the water road workers brought to the job in summer. The state granted the grievance and supplied ice to roads crews in Washington, Allegany, and Garrett Counties, even though Garrett County was still unorganized.

"When I got to Garrett County," said Metz, "guys looked me in the face and said, 'We aren't drinking none of your [chilled] union water.'"

Bennie Beckman, a Swanton [Garrett County] resident, was hired by the state roads in 1960, after a short stint as a fireman on the B&O Railroad. He began working as a laborer and moved up to equipment operator, truck driver, and grader operator before retiring as a Garrett County foreman in 1991.

"I helped Ray Metz organize [in the early 60s]," said Beckman. "We had a good organization. Ray knew the ropes. But it was hard to get anything accomplished because about half the workers belonged to the MCEA. We wanted more than the state offered, but MCEA made it hard to organize against the state."

Despite the divisions and roadblocks, state highway workers made advances. From its formation, members of the Association in Garrett County had compared their wages, benefits, and treatment to their peers' compensation on the state roads.

Organizer Michael Lindner was at the clandestine meetings between AFSCME and the Garrett County roads employees' delegation. He even moved his family camping trailer up to Garrett County, where he could stay after long organizing days.

Organizing county road workers, "was a struggle all of the time," said Metz. "I was working [for the state roads], too. I was up in Garrett County on my own time. Mike Lindner and I became good friends. I stayed in his trailer, and we complained about each other's snoring. Mike had good rapport with people up there."

Lindner and Metz were supported and mentored by Alva Lewis, who convened the road workers' Cumberland organizing meeting as head of the Western Maryland Central Labor Council. As president of United Rubber Workers Local 26 at Kelly-Springfield Tire in Oakland, Lewis was hired by AFSCME to serve as both spokesman and mentor for the road workers.

Elbert Lewis, Alvah Lewis's nephew, said, "Alva was born in Tucker County, West Virginia. He wasn't an educated man. He got what he got [knowledge] from work and sweat so he could sit across the table from the men with the education. He had an insurance agency in Frostburg. He also plowed gardens for side income all around Frostburg."

"I had a lot of respect for Alva," said Metz, praising the AFL-CIO leader's street smarts and competence. Metz said the husky, 6-foot rubber worker was a good union man and negotiator and especially keen at arbitration. "Alva Lewis and Mike Lindner inspired me to get involved."

Hubert Friend: "Show Us Who Supports the Union"

On October 6, 1969, Michael Lindner attended a Garrett County Board of Commissioners meeting to report that members of the road employee's association had approved AFSCME representation. He asked the board for union recognition.

Hubert Friend asked Lindner for a list of names of employees who were supporting AFSCME. Linder told him the names could only be supplied "through an intermediary." Friend replied that road workers were already working under an agreement signed with their association. He said the "AFSCME matter" could be discussed in June 1970 upon expiration of that agreement.

113

Ross Sines accused Lindner and his organization of being "only interested in collecting dues." Lindner responded that, while dues were "a consideration," the main goal of the union members who requested AFSCME affiliation was to "negotiate a better contract."

The commissioners decided to "take no action" and considered the matter [of AFSCME recognition] to be "dropped for the present at least."

But AFSCME didn't consider it "dropped." On December 8, Ernie Crofoot and Michael Lindner appeared before the commissioners accompanied by road worker Wellington "Jack" Sowers. They notified the board that 95 percent of the road workers had signed a petition requesting a change in representation from the Association to AFSCME.

The minutes of the December 8 meeting state: "There was considerable discussion on the availability of names of employees requesting the change in representation."

Crofoot told commissioners the names on the petition could not be revealed. But he said they could be made available to a "neutral party such as a minister or priest for checking against a list of signatures of road workers."

Hubert Friend suggested that residents Wesley Schaible, executive vice president of Garrett National Bank, and George Littman, First National Bank of Oakland board member, be allowed to see the list if they were willing. He said the "present system of bargaining with roads employees is working well and we [Sines and Friend] would like to see it continue."

Despite having suggested that Schaible and Littman review the petition, Friend again asked to see the list. Sines said the board and the road workers should continue to "work out their problems as in the past [through the Association]." He opposed dues check-off, providing for automatic per capita payments to the union from the county.

Sines suggested the union would not "be of advantage" to workers because no more money would be available from the county budget and union dues for the workforce would total $6,000 a year.

The dues, Sines contended, would "reduce the amount for road workers to spend."

Paugh said he believed the commission "ought to give the men a chance [to recognize the union]," suggesting a "disinterested and impartial person" be allowed to check the names of men who signed the list.

Michael Lindner, Crofoot and a few county employees returned to the commission on the 15th of December. W. Dwight Stover, the commission's attorney, asked Crofoot if road workers were advised the commissioners are not required to recognize a union. Crofoot said the members were aware of that fact, but told Stover the workers "had a right to select their own representation."

Friend introduced a motion stating the board retained "exclusive rights to negotiate with all employees of the Garrett County Roads Department rather than with AFSCME."

With the confidence of wide support from co-workers for affiliation, four representatives of the road workers—Jack Sowers, Harold Riggleman, H. Lowdermilk and Ernest Friend—met with the three Garrett County commissioners on March 2. The minutes state the parties had a "brief discussion of matters concerning the roads department employees and the board." The parties agreed to meet again on March 20, at the commissioners' offices.

Garrett County Commissioners Deny Recognition

There is no record of a meeting taking place on March 20, 1970. Both sides were dug in. Sines and Friend refused to recognize AFSCME, while the union demanded to be recognized as the legitimate representative of the road workers. No middle ground. Paugh, too, rejected a middle ground and continued to support the association's right to affiliate with AFSCME.

[1] Slater, p. 164

10

1970: A NATIONAL WAVE OF STRIKES

"People are trapped in history and history is trapped in them."
- James Baldwin, *Stranger in the Village*

On March 18, 1970, just after AFSCME Local 1834 made their final request for recognition, U.S. Postal Service workers in New York City began a wildcat strike against the federal government. By March 25, 200,000 postal workers had struck nationwide.

The cataclysmic postal strike rocked the nation and its freshly inaugurated president Richard Nixon. Road strikers and their union leaders watched the conflict unfolding on their television sets.

Like the Garrett County road workers, many U.S. postal workers were paid so poorly they qualified for food stamps. They were denied the right to collectively bargain and to strike. Congress had stalled on granting the workers a 5.4-percent raise, though they had voted themselves a 41-percent boost in salaries the year before. President Richard Nixon, who had taken office just three months prior, ordered 23,000 members of the U.S. Armed Forces to sort and deliver the mail.

Strikebreaking failed. Eight postal unions won an immediate 6-percent raise. Congress initiated the Postal Reorganization Act that granted postal workers another 8-percent raise. More significantly, postal workers won the right to collectively bargain with the federal government, with compulsory arbitration if they failed to reach agreement.

In the first nine months of 1970, with U.S. union membership hovering just under 25 percent, there were more than 5,000 work stoppages across the nation, including a "sick-out" by air traffic controllers.

In Cleveland, where several of the road strikers had worked, Teamsters and Rubber Workers struck, drawing support on the picket lines from some Kent State University students who were massing against the Vietnam War. On May 4, 1970, four student war protestors were killed and nine injured during an assault by the National Guard, drawing international attention.

Five million workers faced contract expirations that year, two million more than in 1969. The wage and benefit increases they won outstripped those of prior years, averaging 10 percent, two points higher than the prior year. [1]

The broadly publicized strike and boycott in support of the United Farmworkers came to a victorious end as growers signed contracts with the union, and workers in Pennsylvania won a labor relations act governing public workers.

There have been no surveys or polls to discern whether or how these national developments influenced the Garrett County Road workers Strike of 1970. Perhaps the Garrett County road workers were ready to break out of their parochialism by joining an international union. Perhaps the workers shared President Nixon's perspective: "Once you get into this great stream of history, you can't get out."

[1] *Monthly Labor Report*, Volume 94, Jan. 1971

11

THE STRIKE IS ON

Picket Lines are Drawn

"The only thing workers have to bargain with is their skill or their labor. Denied the right to withhold it as a last resort, they become powerless. The strike is therefore not a breakdown of collective bargaining—it is the indispensable cornerstone of that process."

— Paul Clark

On April 7, as the first calves of the season were being delivered in farms across the county, 10-year-old Chris Crabtree was living directly behind the county road department's garage on Garrett Highway (Rte. 219) in Oakland. Knowing that WMSG Radio paid $25 for news tips, he called the station and collected his fee for being the first to report on the picket lines he saw forming outside the garage.

Thirty-six years later, Crabtree joined the roads department and was elected treasurer of AFSCME Local 1834.

In addition to the picketers Crabtree saw gathered in Oakland, striking road workers set up lines at county garages in Grantsville, Friendsville and the county's quarry at Sang Run, demanding the commissioners reverse their opposition to recognition. The work stoppage was the fourth AFSCME strike for union recognition in Maryland.

Citing AFSCME leader Michael Linder, The *Baltimore Sun* reported that 139 out of 144 road workers had struck, with five remaining home but not participating in the work stoppage. The *Sun* said county commissioners reported a lower number [than the union] of workers refusing to report to work.

In an emergency session, Sines and Friend advised strikers

they would be fired if they did not return to the job by April 13. Any employee reporting off sick on April 13 would be required to present a certificate from a Maryland doctor that he was too ill to work. No accumulated overtime hours would be allowed to road workers after April 6.

All but 13 of the workers refused the back-to-work order. Their refusal set in motion a confrontation that turned the quiet county — until then so different from neighboring Allegany County and its organized labor tradition — into a union battleground not unlike the United Mine Workers turf in Harlan County, Kentucky.

The next day, *The Republican* reported that road workers had met in Accident with five "professional union organizers," who, "County Board of Commissioners President Hubert Friend said [incorrectly], were from the Teamsters union."

The Republican echoed the commissioners' skepticism on the depth of AFSCME's support. The paper reported there had been "no vote to strike" and "It was understood a number of the workers were not sympathetic [to striking] but stayed home because they would not have been allowed to cross picket lines."

The commissioners convened another emergency meeting to discuss the strike. County lawyer W. Dwight Stover advised the commissioners that under Article 25 of the Maryland Code, the commissioners have the "authority and duty" to maintain the county's roads. He advised that the strike was "contrary" to the county's current agreement with the road employees' association. Stover argued that since the road workers were public workers under Maryland Case Law, and the Maryland Assembly barred public worker strikes, the strike was illegal.

Still maintaining that their agreement was with the Association, Stover, Sines and Friend directed all their legal efforts at AFSCME Local 1834, the very entity Friend apparently couldn't name and Sines and Stover would not recognize.

The Legal Battle

In 1968, when Baltimore Mayor Tommy D'Alesandro's injunction had little effect on AFSCME's three-day strike, the mayor

119

was forced to negotiate and recognize the union. One year later, despite the Harford County attorney's pledge to prosecute road workers for their sit-in at the county's chambers, the county ended up bargaining with AFSCME. Legal obstacles may have been a hindrance to AFSCME, but they were not stopping its organizing campaigns.

As the Garrett County road workers gathered on the picket lines, the union's Baltimore lawyers Herbert Belgrad and William Engleman prepared for another legal battle with the commissioners and their attorney, W. Dwight Stover.

It's unclear that Garrett County's commissioners had given much thought to the legal strategy to defeat the strike. They were blithely dismissive of AFSCME's influence and focused on deciding how much to pay farmers for sheep killed by dogs. Stover looked for legal strategies to shut down the strike, but he would find no worthy precedent to follow.

Private sector strikes and collective bargaining had been subject to extensive judicial review that escalated after the formation of the National Labor Relations Board during the New Deal. Private sector workers had broad rights to strike.

But the NLRB did not cover public worker bargaining. And even FDR had vehemently rejected the right of public workers to withhold their services from the jurisdictions they served.

In a 1937 letter to the National Federation of Federal Employees, Roosevelt wrote: "Militant tactics have no place in the function of any organization of Government employees … looking toward a paralysis of Government by those who have sworn to support it is unthinkable and intolerable."

The nation's political leaders had overwhelmingly condemned public worker strikes since a 1919 strike by Boston's police officers that resulted in chaos in Beantown. Their strikebreaking tactics in the public sector always relied as much on politics as legalities.

In contrast to private sector economic strikes — where the unions' leverage is the loss of profits — public worker strikes are inherently political. Municipalities are denied services, not revenue. Tax-paying citizens outnumber strikers, unlike the private sector, where workers are the majority. The shutdown of services can empower public sector unions with potent leverage for victory or send them to defeat.

In 1970, only two states, Hawaii and Pennsylvania, had granted public workers a statutory right to strike. In the 1960s the U.S. Bureau of Labor Statistics study of public worker strikes considered the average length of strikes for workers whose duties were classified as "essential," "intermediate" or "nonessential."

The study included a breakdown of strikes where the goal was to establish collective bargaining relationships with no laws in place governing the union-management relationship. The average length of such strikes among "intermediate" workers was 22 days.

Garrett County's AFSCME members, the commissioners and their lawyers were embarking upon a public worker conflict whose length and level of disruption would put them far outside of any recent history.

Legal blows on both sides continued between April and September, involving injunctions, consent decrees, consideration by a grand jury and calls for mediation.

Before September, when electoral politics dominated the final rounds of the confrontation, the parties mostly fought to a draw before Circuit Court Judge Stuart B. Hamill, a jurist with influential roots in the county. Hamill was descended from Judge Patrick Hamill, one of the leaders in Garrett County's formation and a friend of John W. Garrett.

Attorney Tom Dabney called Judge Stuart B. Hamill a "seat-of-the-pants judge" who rendered decisions based "more upon common sense than statute." Nevertheless, Hamill's decisions were very rarely reversed.

"Strikingly," said Dabney, "Hamill was a full-fledged Democrat who had military service under his belt." The fact that Hamill won as a Democrat [in an overwhelmingly Republican county] "speaks volumes," said Dabney. "Hamill was popular at the American Legion VFW and a few other places, too."

Had he not served as a judge, Hamill might have needed Dabney's legal services. His habits were legendary. County sheriffs and the State Police frequently intercepted the intoxicated judge when the local bars closed to give him a ride home. On one occasion, when no Garrett County officers were available to take him home, a call to the State Police for an escort in Cumberland was declined.

Both sides hoped that Hamill's common sense and sobriety would fall on their side of the courtroom.

Stover would try to convince Hamill the "sovereignty" of the county must not be ceded to a union of "outsiders." AFSCME would insist on its right to bargain and strike, holding firm to the statement passed at the union's 1966 convention: "...To forestall [the right] of public employees to strike is to handicap free collective bargaining process ... Where one party at the bargaining table possesses all the power and authority, the bargaining becomes no more than formalized petitioning."

Wives Join the Struggle

On April 13, savoring the gains of their 1969 organizing victory after a three-week strike and sit-in, AFSCME road workers from Harford County joined their Garrett County peers on the picket lines four hours away. Also joining the lines were Garrett County members of the Communication Workers of America (CWA) at C&P Telephone Co., now known as Verizon.

People who have walked picket lines know how important "outside" union support from other workers can be; how it energizes strikers and lifts morale, Not unlike reinforcements from other branches of the military or other nations coming to the aid of fighters in battle.

But building the leverage and the wherewithal to win a strike means fending off any attempt by employers to divide *families* making painful sacrifices for long-term gain.

For instance, during a 1979 strike at Glidden Pigments (SCM), a paint producer in Baltimore, the company sent letters addressed to the spouses of the overwhelmingly male workplace. Managers sought to exploit their fears of living without paychecks to push their husbands back to work.

Would Garrett County's commissioners make similar appeals to the strikers' wives?

Almost exclusively male and coming mostly from urban centers, AFSCME's organizers might have been skeptical about the resolve of the strikers' wives. They may not have known about the influence of miners' wives in the region, both supporting and quelling organizing drives in the 1940s. And it would be years before local historians, including Stephen Schlosnagle and others, looking into the county's history of women's suffrage, would reassess and deepen the gender history of the county.

Testing this, AFSCME organizers encouraged the wives of the all-male roads staff to organize themselves. In short order, the wives built a strong bulwark of support for the strikers that extended from the family kitchen table to the churches, shops and farms.

The first evidence of the union's success in mobilizing spouses was reported in *The Citizen*, describing the wives of strikers marching around the Garrett County Courthouse in response to AFSCME Local 1834 members being served with a back to work order.

Overnight, road worker families who had never met one another were standing side-by-side challenging the men who fired their husbands and fathers. Sines' intransigence was already backfiring as the mass firings inspired a union network spanning hundreds of county miles, an alliance of the progeny of men and women who had braved many economic and geographic adversities.

"Our whole family supported us [during the strike]. I knew some of the road worker's families before the strike. I got to know more during the strike," said Kitzmiller resident Donna Evans, wife of striker Rodger Evans. Four years later, she began working at Garrett Manufacturing Co. in Deer Park as a member of the International Ladies Garment Workers Union.

Tom Holler is the son of road worker Lyden Holler and himself a 35-year roads retiree.

"There was a lot of talk between families of men in all three garages. News travels real fast if you just tell the truth," said Holler, who recalled cold mornings, standing around a fire in a barrel on the picket line with his dad.

❋ ❋ ❋ ❋

On April 16, AFSCME purchased a full-page in *The Republican* entitled "Open Letter to Our Neighbors and Friends in Garrett County from the Garrett County Roads Employees."

The letter was signed by 130 road workers, including 19 from the Sang Run quarry, the remainder from the garages—64 from Oakland, 17 from the Accident, and 30 from Grantsville. The letter claimed 139 out of 144 voted to be part of AFSCME Local 1834.

The letter recapped 15 years of the county association's dealings with commissioners, stating, "…too often we were duped, given promises that were not kept and forced into terms that were not to our benefit."

Listing Maryland counties where AFSCME had already been recognized, the letter continued, "We are not asking for more pay at this time. We want our professional negotiators to handle our problems in the future."

The letter emphasized the road workers' concern for the community, a narrative the union would revisit throughout the strike: "We could have called this strike two months ago when the snows were heavy. We could have tied up the whole county then by not plowing the roads, but we didn't. We respected your needs. We kept the roads open so that all of our children could get to school and you could go to work."

George Phillip Lakoff, the cognitive linguist and philosopher born in 1941, has written about the way repetitive narratives shape our brains' neurons and our individual approaches to politics and events. He advises agents of change to carefully frame their messages in light of contradictory values of people who may be "liberal" on some issues and "conservative" on others.

The 1970 strike was profound in its dueling narratives. AFSCME simply could not have prevailed in the conflict without the sophisticated honing of a sharp message that made sense in a place with deep rooted suspicions of "outsiders" and "liberals."

Noreen Mellick Lidston, the daughter of Harford County AFSCME Council 67 organizer Lou Mellick, remembers her father criticizing union members in Garrett County for not striking in the winter, when idle snowplows could have brought the county to a halt. But the very timing of the strike was a key element in Local 1834's messaging, one attuned to the values of the more insular county.

Months into the strike, Wellington "Jack" Sowers, the charismatic president of Local 1834, told AFSCME's magazine, *The*

Public Worker, "We had an ace in the hole. We could have struck during the January snows. If we had known what we know now about public support, we would have used our ace. But we didn't want to hurt the school children, so we decided to hold off until March."

Sowers, a part-time horse trainer and member of the National Guard, balanced his care for his neighbors with militant warnings to those who would break the strike. "We'll go to knuckle junction if that's what it takes to prove a point," Sowers told *The Public Worker*, which described him as the union's 35-year-old "tobacco-chewing" local president.

On April 16, AFSCME members working on the state roads joined members of the CWA at C&P Telephone Company, picketing alongside Local 1834 members.

Sines repeated his opposition to dues check-off. He and Friend released a statement that under existing statute and case law, "the commissioners *cannot* recognize the union."

Sines and Friend told *The Republican* the roads employees' association had signed a two-year agreement in June 1968 containing the following wage rates: labor $1.97; light operators $2.10; chauffeurs $2.37; operators $2.44; shop foreman $2.50.

In addition, the agreement provided for 13 holidays, hospital insurance and 30 days of sick leave.

The commissioners said the workers' failure to *honor their agreement* was the cause of their firings. Sines said 12 men had reported for work but were turned away by pickets. Paugh agreed the contract with the Association was in effect. But he repeated his call for settling the strike. From Cumberland, Alva Lewis said the union was ready to sit down with commissioners.

Sines Tells Ministers: "You Save Souls. I'll Save the County"

On April 12, members of the Mountaintop Ministerial Association, concerned about the status of family members and parishioners who worked on the county roads, attended the Board of Commissioners meeting to discuss the the strike. They had previously attended a meeting of union members.

The ministers were broadly representative of the county's leading religious congregations listed in the 1980 Census: 26 Unitedist, 12 Assemblies of God, 10 Church of the Brethren, and 9 Evangelical Lutheran.

Revs. James Remley and Thomas Crogan led a group of seven Protestant clergymen: Donald Green, Lawrence Sherwood, John Grant, Eugene Thayer, Vaughn Taylor, Donald Matthews and George Tichinel.

They presented the commissioners with a resolution: "The [ministerial] Association will be willing, at the invitation of both the County road workers and the Board of Commissioners, to help in any way that is mutually agreed upon by all Parties involved in finding a peaceful solution to the present problem."

Looking back, Sines said, "One [minister] Rev. George Tichinel did all the talking. He was a union man from the coal mines. I told him, 'It's your job to save souls. It's my job to take care of the county.'" Tichinel was the only minister "really with the strike," added Sines, who didn't recall the other preachers coming before the commission.

The Citizen featured Sines' retort to the ministers in a headline: "Ministers Rebuffed…You Save Souls…We'll Run County…Say Commissioners." The ministers refuted Sines' charge they were trying to "settle" the strike or interfere with the commissioners, contending they were on a "fact-finding" mission.

"I believe my dad would have supported the strikers," said Rev. Daryl Tichinel, George Tichinel's son. Born and raised in the area of Mt. Zion Road in Swanton, George Tichinel went to work in coal mines on George's Creek in Allegany County and Vindex (Garrett County). After swearing off liquor, he became a part-time preacher at the Walnut Bottom Assembly of God church.

"My dad was an advocate for the union because of the wages," said Rev. Tichinel, who said his father talked about work days for which he was not paid due to low yields on coal, his debts building up in the company store. "If my dad believed in something, you wouldn't shut him up."

George Tichinel's brother Martin served as spokesman for the road employees' association and ran the road department's grader, maintaining streets that were heavily used by vehicles hauling coal close to the family's homes.

126

Despite their differences over labor issues, a year before the strike, Sines and Rev. George Tichinel traveled with some Garrett County ministers to Baltimore to oppose teaching sex education in Maryland's public schools.

County Residents Apply for Work During Strike

Final paychecks were issued to road workers on April 23, covering wages for one day, April 6. Alva Lewis reiterated that the strike was "not about wages but ...union recognition and dues check-off."

The commissioners repeated that they "cannot" recognize the union but would continue to talk to the Association regarding a new contract. The union filed a bill of complaint against the commissioners asking for a permanent injunction to end "discrimination" against the union.

The commissioners received applications from workers willing to work during the strike, but none had yet been hired. Lawrence Bernard was one of the men who applied for work.

Bernard reported, "The commissioners ran an ad in the paper [for road workers during the strike]. I was a mechanic for Clayton Arnold Bros. Farm Equipment. The commissioners called me in for an interview. I had nothing against any of the guys who wanted a union, but I needed a job."

Union Issued Show Cause Order

On April 27, Circuit Court Judge Hamill gave the union until May 15 to "show cause" for their strike. A union official stated that the union planned to circulate petitions throughout the county asking for Sines' and Friend's impeachment. He accused them of misappropriating tax dollars by continuing to pay salaries to men who had agreed to cross picket lines, despite their not performing any work on the roads.

The commissioners and Stover met with a union delegation that included AFSCME organizers Michael Lindner and Alva Lewis alongside road workers Henry Trickett, Jack Sowers, James Faidley,

Calvin Rinker, Ernest Friend, and Hollie Atwood.

"Before he was hired on the roads, my husband worked in mines in Pennsylvania and Allegany County," said Doris Atwood Ray, married to Hollie Atwood during the strike. Her husband was born in North Carolina where his family worked a small farm.

"He was used to making more money [in the mines]," said Ms. Ray. "But the county was steady income, and it was feast or famine in the coal mines."

Ernest Friend is prominently featured in the foreground of photos from the strike, his arms crossed, serious and sturdy, wearing a plaid short-sleeved shirt.

"My father worked in small coal mines [before he was hired on the roads]. One of the mines was in Kitzmiller. He was on his knees all the time," said Ernest Friend's son, Gary. "During the strike, Dad walked the picket line every day. We had food stamps and Dad would pick up work around Deep Creek Lake cleaning up a lot or putting a boat dock in the water."

In a final attempt to prevent chaos and preserve the commissioners' relationships with Ernest Friend, Hollie Atwood and the other leaders at the commission meeting, Paugh made a motion to recognize AFSCME. Hubert Friend told Paugh and the union members, "You have taken the matter to court, so that is where it will be decided."

Stover cited a Maryland Court of Appeals case – *Mugford vs. Mayor and City Council of Baltimore* – that held the governing body of Baltimore could *not* recognize a union; that union membership could only be recognized on behalf of individual members. Further, dues check off would only be instituted if deductions for other purposes such as organizations like the United Fund and the Red Cross were also allowed by the employer.

The two commissioners ordered final paychecks totaling $67,000 to be ready for distribution to terminated workers. Only a few workers showed up for their checks. The rest were mailed out.

Sit-In At the Courthouse

While their union representatives met with the commissioners, strikers, their wives and supporters conducted a sit-in in the rotunda at the Garrett County Courthouse. Nadean Whitacre, the wife of striker Sheldon Whitacre, recalls supporting the strikers at the Garrett County Courthouse until her then three-year-old son "got rowdy."

The Citizen reported that after the State Police arrived, the crowd began to move forward. According to the newspaper, AFSCME representative Wilford Stoll tried to keep the group from surging forward. Stoll was sprayed with mace, arrested and charged with assaulting a state trooper. He was released on $100 bond. Charges were quickly dropped on the former Marine and machinist on the B&O.

Helen Haenftling Fike joined the other women at the courthouse. Her husband Jim and her father Leonard Haenftling were strikers. "The union said, 'Gather up some women.' And the [commissioners] found out that the women stuck with the men," said Fike, an Accident resident. The women blocked all doors of the courthouse at the end of the workday. Friend called the deputy sheriff to move them aside.

Fike reported, "They [commissioners] didn't want to talk to the women. Period. We were there if the men needed us. This was no fun. It was a nerve-wracking thing."

Her mother-in-law was supported by welfare after her husband died when Jim Fike was 16 years-old. Jim swore never to rely on public assistance. He and Helen built their house together. Helen gathered stone in the nearby woods and the couple lived in the basement until Jim and his brothers, carpenters by trade, helped finish the home.

Virginia Rowan Nazelrod, wife of striker Eugene Nazelrod, joined the protest. During her husband's WWII service, Virginia, the daughter of a coal miner, worked at Mt. Airy Canning Co. in Loch Lynn, outside of Oakland. She had a second job as a cook at the William James Hotel, a vacation residence for U.S. presidents.

Their son Curtis Nazelrod said his mother was offered jobs by visiting U.S. presidents as a White House cook, but never took them up on the offer.

"She did everything she could do to help win the strike,

including working in the strike store [distribution center],'" said her son, who, along with his siblings, pushed his parents to let them participate in the strike.

"I remember my parents being real concerned about us getting hurt," said Nazelrod, who was 12 years-old at the time. "My dad said he didn't want us involved, but we convinced him we would stay in the truck and watch out to help keep him safe."

The younger Nazelrod remembers holding a shotgun in the truck "in case there was trouble," and working in the union's distribution center. On one occasion, he joined his father and other strikers, asking a crew employed at Buffalo Coal's strip mine to cease making repairs on public roads during the strike. "They complied," said Nazelrod. "They were very supportive of the strike after we talked to them."

The Republican reported: "Numerous couples applying for marriage licenses were startled by the protests at the courthouse." The paper reported Sheriffs' deputies "escorted Sines and Friend from their offices in the building to their homes."

Striking workers followed Hubert Friend to his home. Friend told reporters that several times during the night strikers would pass his home and blow their horns.

"My mom used to get phone calls during the strike and people would be nasty and hang up," said Vera Dunithan, Hubert Friends' daughter. "I was living in Virginia during the strike. I remember coming home for a visit. There were nails in the road, and I got four flat tires."

Five decades after the strike, Ross Sines decried what he saw as the mob mentality of the strikers, citing one example as a personal betrayal. He said he expected Joe Whitacre to oppose the strike. Only months before the strike, Sines hired Sheldon Whitacre, Joe's son, to work on the county roads while Sheldon was still working in Ohio, breaking a rule that said only county residents could be hired.

The senior Whitacre and his son both joined the strike. Joe Whitacre told Sines he was ostracized by his co-workers in the roads employees' association for refusing to join the one-day strike in 1965 and "wouldn't do that again."

12

PRESSURE IS BUILDING UP

A Priest's Lonely Protest

Fr. Paul Byrnes, a native of Lonaconing in Allegany County, learned about the road workers' strike on visits back to Garrett County. Two years earlier he and his mother had built a home on the southeast corner of Deep Creek Lake.

"Social justice was stronger than individual morality at St. Mary's Seminary in [north] Baltimore," said Byrnes, who was ordained in 1962. Challenging injustice was part of his family's story. Byrnes repeatedly heard the narrative of his great grandfather, an Irish immigrant, whom family members said was killed by the owners of the coal company he was trying to organize along George's Creek.

Fr. Byrnes was a first cousin to George Aloysius Meyers, Lonaconing's Communist labor activist, who helped organize workers at the Celanese plant in Cumberland in the 1930s. Meyers, who had graduated from LaSalle High School, run by the Christian Brothers, was elected president of the Textile Workers union at Celanese. After WWII, he joined other unionists building a federation of Allegany County unions. In 1951, Meyers was arrested for violation of the Smith Act, charged with advocating the violent overthrow of the U.S. government and served 38 months in a federal reformatory.

Family members were surprised when he attended the 1999 funeral of his cousin, George Meyers. "They didn't expect a Catholic priest to be mourning a communist," he said.

The Byrnes family identification with workers and their struggles shaped Fr. Byrnes' view of the roads strike. "I was really frustrated that the county commissioners wouldn't settle with the road workers," said Byrnes, who traveled to Deep Creek Lake nearly every weekend.

"I was used to standing up for social justice. I was at the March on Washington with Dr. King in 1963," said Byrnes, who penned a letter to the county commissioners. "I told them I didn't have any children in school and, since they weren't repairing the roads, I wasn't going to pay my taxes," said Byrnes.

After the strike, the new commissioners called Byrnes into their offices and encouraged him to resume paying taxes, saying they "wouldn't want to arrest a priest." He asked if the strike had been settled. When they said yes, he consented to resume payments.

Known for celebrating mass for boaters at his lake home and for skiers at St. Peter's at the Lake, Byrnes recounted his memories of the strike in a 2019 homily at St. Peter's. It was another of his personal and self-deprecating sermons widely praised by full-time parishioners and second homeowners on their Garrett County weekends.

In his blog, *Half Hermit by the Lake*, Msgr. Byrnes, who passed away in 2020, paid his respects to *Catholic Worker* co-founder and pacifist Dorothy Day.

"To me she was like the woman who lived by the river and kept fishing drowning people out of the water," he wrote. "She soon decided to go upstream to stop those who were throwing the people into the river."

On April 28, strikers prevented office personnel from entering the county roads building at the north edge of Oakland. Sines reported that strikers had taken keys to roads department equipment.

When trees were placed across major intersections obstructing traffic, strikers were suspected. A deep hole was blown open by dynamite on White Rock road near Blooming Rose road. Residents partially filled it in. State police interrogated Paul Cosner, a road worker hired in the Sang Run quarry just three years before, about the explosion.

The Western Maryland AFL-CIO launched a strike fund on April 30 to support AFSCME Local 1834. The same day, the front page of *The Republican* featured a photo showing dynamite damage to the bridge over Cherry Creek near Deep Creek State Park.

Road workers Ray Artice and Danny Uphold were arrested for allegedly dynamiting another bridge. "They were suspected," says

Lonnie Artice, Ray's son, "because they were in the same area [as the explosion] cutting pulpwood for a little extra money."

The two road workers were released after being taken to Cumberland and administered lie detector tests. Lonnie Artice said his father and Uphold "were in the wrong place at the wrong time."

The Citizen's weekly editorial solicited canned goods and financial help for the strikers to be delivered to the Western Maryland Central Labor Council's labor temple in Cumberland.

Editor Virginia Rosenbaum wrote: "The Garrett County Road Workers are being subjected to old-time strike-breaking methods that should be part of history … If the workers quit now, there is a question as to whether or not they would even have a job to return to. If they continue, they need your help. Remember that the two Commissioners have ignored your signatures asking them to negotiate."

Union Served with Injunction

Judge Hamill signed a temporary injunction on May 1, restricting the strikers' activities. A hearing was set for May 11. Hamill's writ enjoined workers from picketing various county places of business and from "disrupting or molesting" the department's vehicles or the commissioners and to return all ignition keys to county vehicles.

The court stated: "There is no inherent right of public employees to strike against their governmental employer…"

The writ cited instances of damage to bridges and the "invasion" of the courthouse by strikers and supporters. The road workers were given 15 days to respond. The union countered Hamill's injunction with a bill of complaint asking for a declaratory judgment against the commissioners.

In an extraordinary step for a law enforcement entity, the Garrett County Sheriff's Department issued a show cause order in *support* of the union. The order, signed by Hamill, gave the commissioners until May 10 to answer why they would not grant the *same rights* to AFSCME Local 1834 as enjoyed by the Garrett County Road Employees' Association.

AFSCME representative Wilford Stoll and several women filed a complaint against the State Police for their actions on April 27.

With county attorney Stover on vacation, Sines and Friend hired Cumberland attorney Miller Bowen to represent the commission.

In an editorial, *The Citizen* stated: "Five weeks into the strike … has uncovered some interesting and tragic facts. The most tragic of them all is the fact that 50% of the Garrett County road workers are eligible for food stamps when they are working full time on Garrett County roads … When we talk of 'wasting the taxpayers' money, let's talk about the waste of hiring an Allegany County attorney [Miller Bowen] to help [refute] the charges brought against the county by the union."

"Links in the Chain"

On May 2, a caravan of 62 cars carrying strike supporters entered Oakland for a rally. Ernie "Butch" Crofoot Jr., the son of the Baltimore AFSCME leader, recalled accompanying his father there. The younger Crofoot had quit college in 1967 during his sophomore year at University of Maryland, got married and began working at the B&O Railroad's freight yard.

Crofoot Jr. arrived in Oakland carrying a guitar. On the courthouse steps, he sang "Links in the Chain," a Phil Ochs' song about workers who were "mechanized out of their jobs."

He remembered the "impressive crowd" that had gathered to greet the caravan as he sang: "Come you ranks of labor, come you union core and see if you remember the struggles of before when you were standing helpless on the outside of the door and you started building links on the chain."

Lonnie Artice, son of striker Ray Artice, remembered one of the many union caravans.

"They paraded through Oakland blowing horns around the courthouse. We had a '56 Chevy in the parade," said Artice, who recalled going to the union store that was replenished with goods donated from trade unionists from Baltimore and Cumberland to "pick up Shredded Wheat and toilet paper."

On May 11, The Board of Commissioners, represented by Stover and Bowen, filed a permanent injunction against unionists

Michael Lindner, Wilford Stoll, Alva Lewis, Jack Sowers, Ernest Friend, and other road workers.

The injunction asked that road workers turn over the keys to all county vehicles and cease and desist from disrupting both proceedings at the county courthouse and county roadwork. AFSCME, represented by Baltimore attorneys Herbert Belgrad and William Engleman, asked that the injunction be dismissed on procedural grounds.

Consent Decree Negotiated

On May 14, Judge Hamill leveraged his injunction to negotiate a consent decree. It limited pickets to 20 at each county garage and called for pickets to act peacefully. Another hearing was set to attempt to settle the conflict.

On May 25, a hearing was held on the union demand to be recognized as the workers' exclusive bargaining agent. *The Citizen* reported that 100 people were present during testimony. In cross-examination, AFSCME attorney Engleman established that commissioners were paying 13 non-striking road workers even while the strike was preventing them from performing their jobs.

The men included Owen Bach, Ernest Hauser, Waldo Zinkan, Clement Frazee, Parley Savage, Joseph DeWitt Jr., Jacob Jones, Fred VanSickle, Harry Griffith, Stephen DeWitt, Paul Frazee, Harry Vitez and Claude Fike.

Engleman, seeking to establish Sines' bias against AFSCME, also confirmed the commissioners had been "checking off" dues from road workers' paychecks for the Association. Engleman asked Sines if members of the Association had ever gone on strike. Sines said, "Yes," recalling the one-day work stoppage that took place around the first week of July 1965, the same time he suffered his tractor accident.

Engleman pressed Sines on his earlier statement that it would be "illegal" for the county commissioners to recognize AFSCME. He asked Sines if, in later discussions with the county's attorney, he had been told that the county could recognize the union. Sines answered:

"I have been told that, but I haven't been officially cleared up in my mind yet."

Paugh testified in favor of union recognition. At the conclusion of the hearing, Hamill asked for written memoranda from both parties, giving them until May 28 to submit their arguments.

The Tragedy in Their Lives

"The prosperous dairy and corn farmers with 100 acres or more store their money in the county banks like hay for the winter, looking with distaste and [incomprehension] at those collecting welfare and receiving food stamps, the 4 out of 10 families living on less than $3,000 a year. Infants die here at a higher rate among the white poor than among the black ghetto dwellers in large cities."
- from "Garrett County Insulated to Change from Outside" — Thomas Edsall, *Baltimore Evening Sun*, Sept. 9, 1970

The *Baltimore Sun* was not widely read in Garrett County, where most TV news all comes from Pittsburgh. But the *Sun* and other big city papers dispatched reporters to Garrett County. Many, like Thomas Edsall, focused on the poverty and income disparities in the county before and during the conflict.

Edsall reported that nearly 3,000 county residents out of 21,000 were collecting welfare benefits. And nearly 800 farmers grossed less than $3,000 per year. Meanwhile, assets in both First National Bank and Garrett National Bank had doubled in the previous four years. Looking for validation of the dire economics, Edsall quoted Rev. John Grant, vicar of St. John's Episcopal Church in Deer Park and a respected local historian.

"The people here," said Grant, "don't see the tragedy in their own lives."

Today, when reporters from metropolitan areas file stories from rural settings, their portrayals are widely disseminated. The reporters who showed up in Garrett County in 1970 lent some gravitas to the confrontation. It's unclear what residents made of their down-and-out descriptions of the county and its people. The dominant and persuasive interpretations of the strike came from two Garrett County newspapers.

Comparing syndicated columns in *The Citizen* and *The Republican*, one might expect their publishers to have taken similar positions on the roads department strike. Back in the 1970s, neither paper sought to "balance" political commentaries in the overwhelmingly Republican county, where distrust of the federal and state government ran deep as the abandoned mines.

The Republican, the venerable weekly founded in 1877, featured a regular column by Thurman Sensing of Nashville. Formerly the public relations director of the Southern States Industrial Council, Sensing promoted right-to-work laws, less government regulation of business and an end to the "interference" of the federal government in civil rights.

Garrett County surveyor M. Virginia Rosenbaum purchased The *Allegany Citizen* and renamed it *The Citizen* in 1961. She published the libertarian upstart until 1983. Rosenbaum's paper gave voice to John J. Synon, a vocal supporter and biographer of former Alabama Governor George C. Wallace. In an April 17, 1969, column in *The Citizen*, Synon attacked popular anchor David Brinkley of NBC's Nightly News for asking viewers to "put our faith in two institutions, labor unions and the federal government."

Despite their appeal to political conservatism in the wake of the Civil Rights Act of 1964, *The Republican* and *The Citizen* took fundamentally different paths in their reporting on the strike.

The dominant and well-financed *Republican* decried the strike's disruption of the county's stability. The paper criticized the stubbornness of the commissioners. But it also cautioned against giving AFSCME "union shop" status where all workers would be "coerced" to join the union and decried threats of violence by strikers if they were not rehired. *The Republican* printed long letters to the editor from former Republican State Senator Clifford Friend (1896-1994) opposing the strike, letters by strike supporters, and ads purchased by both the union and its adversaries.

The Citizen lambasted Sines and Friend for opposing the union, even suggesting a taxpayer revolt because the commissioners were still paying men who vowed to work during the strike but hadn't yet been employed. *The Citizen* said any violence against people or property was the inevitable result of commissioners who lacked respect for the men who worked for them.

Libertarian Firebrand Virginia Rosenbaum

Born in 1921 in Suffolk, Virginia, Rosenbaum was descended from the Hinebaugh family, which settled in Garrett County in the early 1800s. She grew up outside of Washington, D.C., attending school in Bethesda, Maryland and then Strayer's Business College.

After brief careers as a real estate broker, paralegal and journalist, Rosenbaum moved to Garrett County, settling in Finzel, near the border of Garrett and Allegany Counties. Prior to her arrival, the area had been a pivotal one in the county's politics, with road worker Asa Wilhelm and his extended family wielding influence in Republican politics.

Rosenbaum followed suit, always combining her writing with face-to-face confrontations.

In 1969, before the roads strike, Rosenbaum showed up at a commission meeting to complain about the condition of the roads in her electoral district. She said residents were thinking of putting their taxes in escrow if the roads weren't repaired, saying the county needed to support the residents' "Get the People out of the Mud" program. Friend, Sines, and Paugh said they would address the problems.

Rosenbaum's coverage of the strike far exceeded the request of road worker Eugene Nazelrod to "report objectively." Her comprehensive coverage of the strike, her pugnacious and uncritical support for the strikers and her criticism of Sines and Friend as men stuck in a prior agrarian era, turned *The Citizen* into a de facto "shop" paper that inspired the strikers to hold out.

Rosenbaum explained her pro-union posture in a June 18, 1970, editorial. She wrote: "Your editor has had considerable experience with labor unions in that she was personnel secretary for the Kelly-Springfield Tire Company [Cumberland, Md.]."

In that capacity, wrote Rosenbaum, "she took all negotiations between Local 26 [Rubber Workers] and the company in shorthand and transcribed them; and in general, worked with the question of labor for many years…"

In an August 6 editorial, Rosenbaum compared the confrontation between strikers and strikebreakers to another scene "witnessed forty years earlier when just a child." It happened at the Taylor Tin Mill in South Cumberland, said Rosenbaum. "People lined both sides of the streets yelling 'scabs, scabs,' at the men marching down the middle of the street to work under police escort."

The ties Rosenbaum built with road workers certainly helped sell her paper. But the relationships she nurtured were also useful to someone who had run successful campaigns for surveyor in past county elections and would win again, running unopposed in 1974. It was an axiom of county politics that victory was best assured with support from the county's road workers, the sheriff's department, and the Farm Bureau.

No exchange of vitriol during the roads strike was more biting than the feud between Rosenbaum and Martha Glotfelty, the county roads department's bookkeeper and a former member of the Maryland House of Delegates.

Rosenbaum criticized Glotfelty in an August 6 column, directly following the confrontation between the strikers and commissioners on the Oakland town parking lot. Rosenbaum wrote that after Glotfelty lost her House of Delegates seat to B.O. Aiken in the previous election, she landed a job in the office of the County Roads Garage and, "from this vantage point, it appears she has been aiding the two Commissioners to the best of her ability in their 40-year-old thinking."

Glotfelty has been "deemed an 'agitator' by many with whom your editor talked," added Rosenbaum. "It's a fact, Mrs. G., "Your kind of thinking is arcadian and has no place in today's fast-moving, modern world."

On Sept. 22, Glotfelty struck back at Rosenbaum, purchasing a half-page "letter to the editor" in *The Republican*. She recounted her status as a secretary stuck in the "lowest pay scale" despite being "the only one who has attended College."

Recalling her attendance at the battle of the bus, Glotfelty described seeing a man [at the Oakland parking lot] "whom I presumed was from Baltimore," yelling through a big horn. "I spoke up to him and said, "Don't you have enough trouble in Baltimore without importing it to Garrett County?"

Glotfelty said, "A State Trooper walked over to me and advised me to say nothing more. I did as he asked me to do. If that is the reason she [Rosenbaum] has called me an 'agitator,' it seems rather exaggerated, don't you think?

"I have been called everything from a 'scab' to a 'communist,'" wrote Glotfelty. "I have been a target for name calling, threats etc. from the strikers and their wives… Fact: A new low in human behavior has been set in this County."

While outspoken in support of the roads strikers' battle for union recognition, Rosenbaum often mirrored the politics of her columnists, defending small businesses against government regulation. Her sharp critique of bureaucrats was part of her success as a libertarian political activist before and after the roads strike.

"Virginia had a voice that could pierce through any number of conversations and she was already a certified character when I met her in 1971," said Tom Dabney, an attorney who arrived in Garrett County that year from Baltimore. "She had things she wanted to say, and nobody else would publish them, so she did. Her column had a flavor of her personal opinions and stories about local people, mostly from up around Finzel."

"Virginia was almost always accompanied by her husband, she called DBA (for Dearly Beloved Angel) in her newspaper," said Dabney. "She was a large woman and had a vintage-1940 hairstyle, bobbed in the back, slightly flared on the sides, wrapped up into the back of her head. She had a pencil stuck in her hair and she wore Miami Beach glasses without rhinestones."

"Virginia wasn't the typical stay-at-home mom," said Jim Raley, a subsequent Garrett County commissioner, who, in his youth, cut Rosenbaum's lawn. "She had a dirt speed-track by their house. Cars were racing. She did surveying, ran a newspaper, the dirt track and a small farm, too."

Pointing to his upper chest, Ernie Gregg, a retired Oakland pharmacist and six-term Garrett County commissioner, said, "There's probably a hole here where Virginia [Rosenbaum] kept poking me."

Before the roads strike, Gregg had served on the Oakland City Council that had just approved fluoridation of the town's water. Virginia Rosenbaum had earned a reputation as one of the nation's most strategic, effective opponents of water fluoridation. "You are poisoning your kids," she told Gregg, whom she nevertheless supported in later elections.

Perhaps Rosenbaum's editorial of May 21, 1970 best reflects the vision and goal that drove her to give such extensive coverage to the strike: "The voters of this County will have to realize that Garrett County is opening up…that it is no longer made up of a small town at the Northern part of Maryland, completely isolated from the hustle and bustle of today's world, run for the benefit of a few men who carry $100 bills in their pockets while the rest of the men work full-time for a wage which makes them eligible for government subsidies in the way of food stamps, controlled by one ultra-conservative press [*The Republican*] which, in turn, caters to those who carry the $100 bills. Garrett County needs progressive people to run it…remember this at election time!"

Fix The Roads!

On June 22, the minutes of the commission recorded the first appearance before the board by residents complaining about bad road conditions during the strike. Leaving the plowing and spreading manure across their fields, local farmers vigorously demanded action on the strike. Mr. and Mrs. Saylor, residents of lake property, asked for their roads to be repaired and for the union to be recognized.

Virgil Sines appeared on Aug. 10, complaining about the condition of River Road. He was joined by a "Mr. Henshell" who was dissatisfied with the maintenance of a drainage ditch.

Ervin and Walter Broadwater called attention to roads in the New Germany area. Floyd McIntyre and Ronald Stemple raised similar issues. One week later, county insurance agent B.I. Gonder went on record asking for a "settlement of issues" that were obstructing proper maintenance of the roads. On October 5, Paul George, Wilbur Close, and Robert Beachy joined the voices of constituents asking for action on the roads.

"Potholes were everywhere," said Tom Gearhart, a Grantsville resident, who returned from the Army service during the strike. "People realized how much work the road workers did and how they did it."

Lowell Bender visited Hubert Friend at his home to complain about potholes and policy. Hard-pressed road workers and their families were asking for assistance from the agency's already stretched resources.

"I told Friend, the strike wasn't my business. But it was getting to be my business," said Bender. "I asked if he would consider a compromise with the union. He was very friendly and kind. But no way was he going to settle."

Opposition to Ross Sines' hardline stance included his brother. David Sines, Ross Sines' nephew, says his father approached Commissioner Sines after a tenant on property he owned hit a hole in the road while driving near Cranesville Road. His father told Ross he "ought to settle the strike," said David Sines.

On June 25, *The Republican* carried a want ad for new roads employees to replace striking workers. The laborers were offered $1.75 per hour and $2.11 per hour after a 30-day probationary period. Forty chauffeurs were offered $2.43 an hour with 15 operators expected to receive $2.64 an hour. Three shop foremen would bring home $2.79 an hour.

By June 26, only one striking worker had changed his mind and applied to return.

13

THE STRIKE DRAGS ON

Commissioners Negotiate with Strikebreakers

Replacement workers and road workers who had refused to strike met with the county commissioners on June 29 to discuss rates of pay and the terms and conditions of employment. Those discussing the new contract included Claude Fike, Paul Frazee, Joseph DeWitt, Jr. and Freddie VanSickle.

The commissioners offered a 7-percent increase in pay, an increase in sick leave to 20 days a year, and an additional 10 days of hospitalization. The board also agreed to increase hospitalization reimbursements and to pay for overtime hours at the regular-time rates.

On July 2, AFSCME published a full-page ad in *The Republican* asking residents to write to the county commissioners and urge them to recognize the union. The ad alleged that county commissioners were asking road workers to sign a "yellow dog" contract, a binding agreement not to join the union as a condition of hiring.

AFSCME recounted that Governor Mandel and local ministers had offered to help settle the dispute. The union reminded readers that the union had a productive collective bargaining relationship with Allegany County and would, if recognized, establish the same relationship with Garrett County.

On July 9, 21 candidates filed for the primary election for county commissioner.

* DISTRICT 1-Republicans: Allen Paugh, William Fitzwater Jr.; Democrats: William Virts, Bernard Guy, Mason Madigan.

- DISTRICT 2-Republicans: Charles Arnold, Samuel Thomas, C. William Turner, Warren Miller; Democrats: Earl Opel, Allen R. Warnick.
- DISTRICT 3- Republicans: John Ross Sines, Arthur Savage, J. Edward Tasker, O. Dale Uphole; Democrats: Theodore Raynovich, James E. Matthews, Ellis O. Cogley, Wayne B. Hamilton, Harvey H. Sines, Asa E. Nethken.

The Republican corrected a statement made in a prior paper that the county's contract with the roads employees' association contained a no-strike clause. No such clause existed.

The 80-car union caravan crossed Deep Creek Lake, past the cabins of vacationing steelworkers from Pittsburgh, arriving in Oakland on July 11, ready to replicate some of the labor solidarity that defined the visitors' region.

Five days later, in a story headlined "Labor Caravan was Orderly," *The Republican* reported that the caravan "formed in Accident and proceeded to a rented building North of Oakland and distributed food and other items."

The cars then traveled "down Third St. to Oak St., then out to the loop at Browning's Foodland, back on Oak St. to the Garrett County Courthouse where a rally was held. After the rally they went to Swallow Falls for refreshments."

"There Will Be Bloodshed" - *The Citizen*

On July 23, Commissioner Paugh wrote to Governor Mandel asking for mediation. The same day, *The Citizen* proposed a taxpayer protest because roads were not being repaired.

Asserted Virginia Rosenbaum, "Commissioners have been told by two policing bodies [state police and Garrett County Sheriff's office] that they "cannot wet-nurse men trying to take other men's jobs and that only limited protection could be given [to strikebreakers]."

If the commissioners persisted in trying to "get men across the picket line," *The Citizen* speculated, "there will be bloodshed, make no bones about that! This has been a peaceful strike so far, but the old-time Union leaders are beginning to say, 'See we told you so.' This peaceful method produced nothing."

On July 27, Governor Mandel said Sines and Friend had rebuffed his offer of mediation. Two days later, an article in the *Baltimore Sun* quoted Jack Sowers, described as "the wiry, tobacco-chewing president of the county road workers' new union."

Said Sowers, "Yup, We're all a bunch of mean hillbillies…Hell, we're not violent people, but we're going to draw some blood if the commissioners try to send some men out to work on those roads."

Another striker, Cecil Welch, 45, described as a "fired [county roads] truck driver," told the *Sun* reporter, "By God, there's one thing about it—I'll fight for my job." The *Sun* said Welch's vow drew a "Yes sir," from Salem Shreve, 51, an Oakland "native and [roads department] laborer for the past 15 years."

The *Sun* reported that the county's National Guard Armory in Oakland was being prepared for "precautionary contingents" of State Police to maintain order if strikebreakers were put on the job.

The *Sun* described Commissioner Paugh as a "burly farmer who has been cast in the role of the county's maverick commissioner."

"There's going to be bloodshed if those two [Sines and Friend] try to break this strike," said Paugh. "Those two won't tell me what they're going to do. But I've been a working man all my life and I'll fight for the working man. I can't blame the men a bit for holding out. I'd fight for my job, too."

The Republican reported on July 30 that Edmond Grovner, Mandel's chief administrative assistant, said the governor would not intervene in the dispute "unless he was guaranteed cooperation on both sides."

Hubert Friend announced the county was ready to put 100 strikebreakers on the job with police escort.

The Republican reported, "Mr. Paugh [commissioner] said yesterday that some 95 percent of the county's school children travel to consolidated schools by bus on the 739 miles of roads which need repair."

Paugh noted that the county was in "excellent state financially and is financially able to give the road workers a raise."

In *The Citizen*'s July 30 editorial, Rosenbaum attacked Sines for continuing to collect taxes to pay for non-striking roads employees who were not working due to the strike. She argued that Sines "trick[ed] the population on taxes" by boasting about reducing the property tax rate by 20 cents per $1,000 of value.

The Citizen contended that Sines knew the state would raise the county's assessment rate, the lowest in the state, neutralizing his promised "savings."

Paugh told the *Baltimore Sun* Sines and Friend asked for the National Guard to be called out to protect replacement workers but were told service members would only be called in an emergency. The *Sun* said newly hired strikebreakers were refusing to begin work until their safety was ensured.

The Sun reported on August 3 that Sines and Friend had rejected a last- minute plan by Joseph J. Biondo, a federal mediator from Pittsburgh, to settle the strike after a two-hour closed-door meeting with Circuit Court Judge Hamill and lawyers representing the county commissioners and AFSCME. The paper said union leaders were predicting violence if the commissioners tried to put replacement workers on the job on August 4.

"The rejected plan," the *Sun* reported, "provided for the striking road workers to return to work immediately and take a further vote on their union affiliation after Election Day in November."

Sines' and Friend's rejection of mediation only strengthened the union's need for a decisive show of force on August 4.

The battle of the bus consumed the county's attention, akin to how the community dealt with the winters' up-to-the-windows snows. The snows were met by the sharing of plow, shovel, and muscle. The dig-outs were a cause for unity, communal meals, a celebration of mutual safety and the common resolve of the people and their leaders.

But digging out of the strike and ensuring safety would be messier and more divisive. Jerry Wurf, AFSCME international president, stated: "Government workers have proved that when they are not dealt with justly, they will defy the law. And they have proved that, in such situations, government is powerless."

Would those words define the next stage of the conflict? If so, who would have the power to get the potholes filled and restore a measure of normalcy to the county?

The day after the parking lot confrontation—with the entire county engulfed in debate and concern over the strike, Governor Mandel and U.S. Senator Joseph Tydings campaigned for re-election in Garrett County.

Governor Mandel and Senator Tydings Visit Garrett County

The *Baltimore Sun* reported that Governor Mandel gave a 10-minute speech on August 5 at Wisp Resort, introduced by William Goldsborough of the state roads commission. The paper reported Mandel didn't mention the roads strike. *The Citizen* featured a photo of Mandel, with Del. B.O. Aiken and Garrett County Democratic Commission candidate Earl Opel, seated at a table.

Senator Tydings, a resident of Harford County, had been elected to the senate in 1964, defeating J. Glenn Beall Sr., a Cumberland native. He was now in a primary election fight with George P. Mahoney, who was attacking him for his support of gun registration.

Tydings visited the county road workers on their picket line at the Accident garage to talk about both the strike and the gun control measure. Democratic Del. B.O. Aiken, also campaigning for re-election, ran an ad in *The Republican* opposing Tydings stance, saying, "I believe that strict enforcement of our laws will do more good than gun registration."

The Citizen displayed a photo of Tydings in Accident and quoted him saying, "When working men get together and want to have a union, they should have that right. It is my understanding that the county recognized the Association, so long as it's called an Association, and when it became affiliated and called itself a Union, it was not recognized and it does not seem to me to be fair… I think the Federal mediator's recommendations should be considered."

The Republican reported that before the governor and senator left town, Commissioner Dick Paugh gave Mandel a painting of a Garrett County farmhouse, produced by county resident Harland Bittinger.

Mandel returned to Garrett County one week later for a labor rally, flying to Allegany County directly from the National Governor's

Conference in central Missouri. The *Cumberland News* reported that 400 people attended the rally, held at the Clarysville Inn, including "a large portion of the striking road workers from Garrett County."

Sines and Friend signed a court order demanding the union show cause why it should not be held in contempt of a prior consent decree, charging that on August 4, "Fifty to 60 pickets had shown up on the Oakland parking lot wearing hard hats and attempted to stop workers from going to work."

Circuit Judge Stuart Hamill scheduled a hearing for September 4. The show cause order listed AFSCME Local 1834, Jack Sowers, Ernest Friend, Michael Lindner, Wilfred Stoll and Alva Lewis.

The Citizen again announced a taxpayers' suit being developed protesting the commission paying strikebreakers who were performing no work.

AFSCME Organizes Adopt-a-Family Effort

In August, AFSCME's national publication, *The Public Employee*, featured an extensive centerfold on the Garrett County roads strike. Several photos of strikers and their families accompanied the article, entitled, "Maryland Mountain Men Fight for Recognition."

The Public Employee interviewed Delwood (Dagwood) Freeland, 45, a 15-year road worker who, with his wife, Betty Jane, had five children and a stepson who was serving in Vietnam.

"The worst thing [about the strike] is the rent," said Freeland. "We're almost four months behind and the landlord has asked us to vacate as soon as possible."

Howard Keefer, a 48-year-old road worker with 22-years on the job, also spoke with the *Public Employee*, telling the paper that he and his wife Joanne lived in a tar paper home—one large room divided by blankets and sheets with two small alcoves. The story said that Keefer took home about $120 for two weeks of work.

Keefer told the paper, "I think the strike is the greatest thing that ever happened. The union is what we need in here in my opinion. A lot of families have children coming on, and if we don't fight now, they will have to do it later on."

A photo of Keefer's family was later incorporated in a collage that was posted in Oakland's county garage. They were pictured on the cover of a brochure for the strike's 20th commemoration at the Wisp Resort and on the wall at AFSCME's Baltimore offices.

AFSCME urged union locals across the nation to "adopt" families like those of Delwood Freeland and Howard Keefer by making monthly contributions of $125 to the union's strike support fund.

Zalman Birnbaum, a Baltimore public relations consultant for AFSCME, organized the adopt-a-family effort. Birnbaum's son, Mark, was just back from service as an Army photographer in Vietnam when his father asked him to join a trip to Western Maryland to take some of the photographs that later appeared in *The Public Employee*.

"My dad loaded the car with food for the strikers and I was welcomed into the strikers' homes," said Birnbaum.

On August 16, the strike became the longest public worker strike in U.S. history. According to the *Washington Post*, the conflict surpassed the previous mark set in 1965 by sanitation workers in Bowling Green, Ohio.

Four days later, a shotgun blast shattered the window of a home owned by William Hugh Brenneman on Jennings Hill Road, Route 495. In the room with Brenneman were Marvin and Leona Beitzel.

The Republican reported that Brenneman had appeared on the parking lot in Oakland the previous week supporting Sines and the newly-hired strike replacement workers.

The Letter to the Editor War

The strike's supporters and opponents battled on the local newspapers' opinion pages. Former State Sen. Clifford Friend opened up the attack on AFSCME in a letter to *The Republican*. He wrote: "Once the Union is designated as a bargaining unit for the men, the Union officers could call strikes because some worthless fellow had been demoted or fired."

Friend was known throughout the county for his fistfight with Garrett County Roads Engineer Webb DeWitt over whether to connect Lakeshore Dr., bordering Deep Creek Lake, with Mayhew Inn Road. The request was said to have come from the influential

149

Naylor family who owned land on the lake. Friend broke DeWitt's jaw and then beat an assault charge in court. Many years later, Lakeshore Dr. was still called "Jawbreaker Road."

"Big unions have written their own record and it is not a pretty one," Friend wrote in an April 30th letter to *The Republican*, decrying "strong armed goons sent to threaten and intimidate public officials." Claiming to advocate for farmers and small business owners, he cited the pay and benefits already achieved by roads workers in the Association: "Our County Roads Workers have no legitimate reason for getting our county tangled up with this kind of outfit [AFSCME]," said Friend. "They are better paid and have more security than most of our self-employed citizens. And they have their homes here, their children are being educated here, their loyalties belong here."

A May 7 letter in *The Republican*, signed by several wives of strikers said: "Mr. Friend was so quick to speak of loyalty. Well these men have a loyalty to this county that he and so many like him could not possibly match or begin to understand … If our husbands can not be granted their constitutional right as American citizens and as citizens of this county to belong to a Union, and be recognized as such, then we are no longer living under a democracy, we are living under a dictatorship."

The letter was signed by Mrs. Thomas Spiker, Mrs. Rodger Evans, Mrs. Harvey Friend, Mrs. Betty Lou Sowers, Mrs Betty Freeland, Mrs. Barbara Guthrie, Mrs. Helen Fike, Pauline Bourner, Lona Ellifritz, Leona Nazelrod, Mrs. Harold DeWitt, Mrs. George White, Mrs, David DeWitt, Mrs. Erma Stephens, Mrs. Howard C. Roth.

Clifford Friend's challenge of the roads workers' "loyalty" to country and county was volatile. Sines was deferred from service in the armed forces, while several strikers and their leaders had served, including Leo Rinker and Eugene Nazelrod, each of whom sustained injuries.

Martha Glotfelty, the county roads department's bookkeeper, also published letters attacking the union. Ridiculing a picket sign saying, "We demand our dignity now," Glotfelty said: "… If he has an honest interest in his work, a desire to do it well, and to find in it some meaning for his daily life, he [the road worker] has already found dignity. With these proper attitudes, he does not need to look for any outside force to confer it upon him." Union members and their wives parried Glotfelty's "outsider" attack with still more letters and ads.

The pens grew even more poisonous as the strike wore on. In an August 13 letter to *The Republican*, Clifford Friend commented on the battle of the bus. "As I understand it," wrote Friend, "there were several dozen state police officers, and our sheriff present when this unlawful destruction of property took place, and neither our sheriff nor any of the state police made any effort to stop the union goons from destroying the bus..."

Lena Nazelrod Bateman, the wife of striker "Skinny" Bateman responded to Friend in the August 27 issue of *The Republican*. "How about all the so-called good sympathizers on the other side. You didn't mention them, Mr. Friend. You said no arrests were made but what about the good law abiding men who were arrested for having guns and loading them to use on our men? Your so-called good citizens attacked our men with meat hooks. There was little said about that. About rape being committed on your people. I'm sure all our men have much better taste than to want any of your inbreds."

In the Sept. 3 issue of *The Republican*, Clifford Friend opposed the union's demand for a "check off" clause, alleging that such a concession to the union would result in the firing of all workers who did not join the strike. Friend wrote: "It is just as difficult to understand why County Commissioner Paugh would lend his support to a scheme that could enslave his fellow citizens, workers, and taxpayers by getting us entangled with a ruthless organization

On Sept. 10, AFSCME purchased a full-page ad in *The Republican*: "Open Letter to Ex-State Senator Clifford Friend." Supporting Paugh's call to recognize AFSCME, the union wrote: "...You [Friend] are again using the BIG LIE when you talk about the union ... Collective bargaining means that both employer and employee sit down together and work out their differences to the mutual advantage of both. This has been done by AFSCME and the Commissioners of neighboring Allegany County. There are 49 AFSCME unions in the State of Maryland, representing more than 17,000 members in State, County, and City Governments."

AFSCME International President Jerry Wurf Visits Oakland

On August 23, AFSCME president Jerry Wurf visited Oakland and was greeted by 90 strikers and their families. Wurf told the crowd, "We're going to see this thing through if you will. Everywhere our folks have stood up and have been willing to sacrifice, we've won. I come to you with no magic and no prophecy of immediate victory. The strike is not just a question of a few cents. It's a matter of human dignity. You look OK. You look like you can take it and you look like you can hand it out."

Wurf presented local members with a $5,000 check from the international union. Wurf then addressed the county commissioners. *The Republican* reported that Sines and Friend sat "stone faced" as he spoke.

Friend told Wurf: "Our position is clear. I have nothing else to say." Sines told Wurf the "majority of people" in Garrett County are opposed to the union and he would continue to represent the majority. Wurf told the newspaper, "I don't understand what is holding up the possibility of dialogue."

AFSCME's *Public Worker* reported that Wurf told the commissioners their position was one that "depends on hunger and privation to prevent the men from making their own choices...This is not the American way of doing things."

Wurf was pictured on the front page of *The Citizen* (August 27, 1970), alongside Jack Sowers and Henry Trickett from Garrett County, Alva Lewis from Cumberland and Wilford Stoll from AFSCME Council 67. Wurf told the press that talking to the commissioners was an "exercise in futility."

Fifty years later, Sines didn't recall Wurf coming to town. But the two men shared more than they each might concede.

Wurf, born in New York City in 1919, contracted polio at age four. Despite a series of operations, he never regained full use of one of his legs and suffered lifelong pain. Wurf's family struggled financially. He joined the Young People's Socialist League and frequently distributed literature on the street, mounting soapboxes to argue with those who were defending the economic and political status quo. [1]

After winning leadership in the union, he gained the reputation of a hard taskmaster, who frequently fired and sometimes rehired staffers.

Sines' family, like Wurf's, had seen financial struggle. Like Wurf, he took pride in his self-reliance. He had suffered pain and lack of mobility after a 1965 tractor accident. His father had been injured in a mine. He was unafraid to use his authority to deny others their livelihood, steadfast in his own righteousness. Years after Wurf had taken to the soapbox in New York City, Sines was still making long drives to Baltimore City to distribute pocket-sized bibles and save souls, mostly in the Black community.

Both men sought to spread their versions of morality in zealous, messianic fashion—Sines in the Anabaptist, anti-government tradition, Wurf in the genre of liberal, Jewish labor solidarity. The critical difference between the two men, squaring off on either side of the nation's longest public worker strike, was in their tactical guile.

Sines was a dogmatist, holding his line and expecting others to follow. Wurf, the kid with the limp leg, the last chosen on the football field, was flexible, always looking for allies, permanent or temporary, who could help put the squeeze on his adversaries.

On August 28, striker Paul Cosner pleaded guilty to "willful and malicious destruction" of the fence surrounding Commissioner Friends' farm on June 16. Circuit Judge Hamill revoked Cosner's $200 bond and ordered him to the county jail.

On September 3, the State Department of Social Services approved public assistance for road workers with children. The recipients were required to be ineligible for unemployment compensation and have no jobs available to them. Union leaders reported that Sines accused many of the strikers of seeking aid under "false pretenses."

The Citizen, featuring a blank check to one of the non-striking workers on the front page, reported that commissioners had already paid $10,000 to no-work strikebreakers.

Publisher Rosenbaum appealed to the fiscal conservatives Sines championed: "Voting for John Ross Sines is approving wasting money," she said. "The pulse of the county will be felt at the primary election on September 15. Even if you are a farmer and have never come in contact with a union, you should know when the handwriting is on the wall. When men organize, it is a reflection that something is wrong."

The Republican reported that Garrett County's registered Democrats had increased their numbers by only 37 voters since 1958. All except two of the county's 20 precincts had Republican majorities.

While Democrats were a distinct minority, many, like Maurice Brookhart, retained significant influence and respect. An early and active member of the Garrett County Democratic Club, Brookhart owned Garrett Truck and Equipment Company and served as vice president of Garrett National Bank.

Born in 1915 in Forest Hills (Harford County, Maryland), Brookhart had traveled to Garrett County during the Depression to work at a CCC [Civilian Conservation Corps] camp in the Big Run, Savage River area. He remained in Garrett County after his CCC service and married Martha Engle, daughter of Ralph Engle, a prosperous north county farmer.

"I think my father was a Democrat because Roosevelt and the CCC saved him," said Brookhart's son, Maurice Brookhart Jr. "He was a generous man who tended to loan money to people who were down and out."

Martha Brookhart, who taught at Grantsville High School before her marriage, worked for the social services board after her children were born. "Amusingly, she was a Republican," said her son.

Farm News Blasts Strike

On Sept. 3, *The Republican* cited excerpts of an editorial in *Maryland Farm News*, published by the Maryland Farm Bureau. The article was headlined: "Unions Use Fear, Loyalty to Achieve Ends."

"Most people have no concept of union pressures unless they live through such experiences [strikes]," the *Farm News* wrote. "Ask the grape growers in California what it has been like to live with the so-called nonviolent farm labor movement, or the Alabama [chicken farmers] about the burning of broiler houses in efforts to organize them.

The *Farm News* continued: "Unions, if allowed to continue their power plays, will easily control our nation because they will be able to stop vital services, including the movement of food from the farm to the marketplace …

"No one will argue against the need for [the] organization of groups of people with similar interest for their own protection and welfare. But, there must be checks and balances if our democratic principles are to survive. The autocracy of business a century ago is now rapidly being replaced with the autocracy of unions. One is as bad as the other."

The Citizen challenged the Farm Bureau's fears of workers organizing. "Most farmers belong to the Farm Bureau, or have connections with it," the column stated. "The National Farm Bureau is about as anti-Union as an organization can get…Knowing little or nothing about the problems of a gigantic farm such as they have throughout the Midwest, and other parts of the country where migrant labor is utilized, we cannot say whether or not a Union is good or bad for a farmer. Around here, it would be practically impossible to organize farm labor. So the problem confronting industry just doesn't apply to a farmer."

In a later issue about the roads strike, Rosenbaum wrote: "Many farmers say if unions come in, taxes will go up. If you're a dairy farmer, you're getting about $6 a pound for milk. How many gallons will you destroy when your milk trucks can't get in because of snow [unplowed because of the strike]? How many tax dollars will you pay in destroyed milk?"

Referencing a recent invitation to labor leaders to attend a Labor Day celebration at the White House, *The Citizen* wrote: "Dick Nixon has sense enough to know that Unions are a necessary way of life."

None of AFSCME's letters to the community appealed directly to farmers, despite their important place in the county and its politics. Rosenbaum's proposal of an alliance between the unions and small farmers was practical. However, building such alliances in the U.S. had largely eluded organized labor since the formation of the Farmer-Labor Party in the 1920s.

On September 4, the "show-cause" hearing was rescheduled to

September 17, after the upcoming primary election. The commissioners included two affidavits from state troopers documenting the union's violation of the prior consent decree by exceeding the number of pickets permitted and carrying sticks and clubs.

Surviving the Strike

Long public strikes cannot be sustained without the physical and emotional support of the surrounding community. Road workers welcomed a wide stream of support from multiple springs.

AFSCME and other unions supplemented the help strikers were already receiving from neighbors and family members. The international union's donations helped keep families in food and clothing. Just as importantly, the support gave them confidence of victory.

Some strikers found new work or simply doubled up on the "side" jobs. Several strikers enjoyed the powerful combination of union solidarity and the bounty of the family farm. Others were grateful for food stamps or help from family with groceries.

Jennings resident Mabel Butler, the wife of Local 1834 member Berman Butler, said her father, a coal miner and farmer, "butchered a cow and saw that we had meat" during the strike.

Mabel Butler's sister Doris Ray, married to leading union member Hollie Atwood, was pregnant at the time. "I was tickled pink that the union supplied baby clothes from a new baby shop in Baltimore," said Ms. Ray.

Terry Rinker, the son of former Local 1834 President Leo Rinker, said, "We ate the fish and deer we killed." It was far more sumptuous fare than Ross Sines' recommendation of "groundhogs and dandelions."

Janet Brant, the wife of striker Harold Brant, who was killed in an industrial accident in the county garage in 1994, said, "I canned. We had a garden and mom gave us meat [from the family farm]."

"I don't remember my father participating in picket lines during the strike," said Frank Vitez, whose father, James Vitez, and uncle George Vitez were strikers. Their brother Harry Vitez was on the list of workers being paid by the county commissioners for refusing to strike.

Self-reliance undergirded the strike. Asa Wilhelm refused all state assistance during the strike. Allen Wilhelm, his son, said, "We only went to the store once a month. I stacked lumber 'til dark after I got home from school. I milked cows. We had milk and cottage cheese and chickens.

"In spring we made ice cream by hand every Sunday. After we got the cows taken care of and wood and the coal buckets were full, then we could do our homework. We had cold water, gravity fed, no inside plumbing, no TV. We had no telephone until Dad got one for his county job [foreman]."

Asa Wilhelm drove a grader at Buffalo Creek Coal Co.'s strip mines during the strike. He had a chance to be hired at Frostburg State College during the conflict, but he stuck out the strike, supplementing his paycheck with food from his farm.

AFSCME marshaled food and clothing collection efforts from labor allies. The Citizen (June 11, 1970) referenced a caravan that "strung out for miles," originating in Baltimore and picking up cars along the way."

The Citizen wrote: "[The cars] carried truckloads of food, including hams for every striking worker, and all kinds of canned goods. Over $2,000 was collected, plus $200 each from Gov. Marvin Mandel and Sen. Joseph Tydings."

The food and clothing were delivered to the union's "store." John Nazelrod, son of striker Eugene Nazelrod, said, "Most strikers were dependent upon the union's store." He said the store was "portable," located for a time on a lot next to the Oakland Garage before moving across from the old Brodax's Market on current Rte. 219.

"The county wouldn't let union members on county property [during the strike] so Mr. Cot Callis [local garage owner] gave us his lot to use."

Victor Nazelrod Jr. said his father worked as a carpenter helping build Bill's Marina on Deep Creek Lake during the strike.

"My dad could do just about anything," said Nazelrod Jr., recalling helping his father a few years before the strike, painting some of the spacious homes on Crook's Crest, overlooking Oakland.

"I was 16 years-old at the time of the roads strike," said Sharon Caple, a retired schoolteacher who grew up in The Cove. Her father, Paul Thomas, built A-frame homes on Deep Creek Lake during the strike.

"My mom had to get food stamps. She hated it," said Caple. "I'm not sure if my father went out to the picket line. He was just quiet about the strike. He wanted to be working."

A growing tourism sector provided opportunities for strikers to make ends meet. "I worked construction with [fellow striker] Ray Artice," said Troy Wakefield, hired only two months before the strike. "We put in a sewage line at Deep Creek State Park."

Union members Ray Artice and Danny Uphold cut pine pulpwood for delivery to nearby sawmills. Leo Miller went to work briefly at the nearby Harbison-Walker brick plant and then worked for Keystone Paving Co. Johnny Tasker, the foreman and striker from Sang Run, helped build a car wash on Route 219 with his brother-in-law. Sheldon Whitacre, newly hired on the roads, worked for Mt. Top Paving during the strike and joined his father, Joe, on the picket line.

Asked by the *Washington Post* how strikers were surviving, Leo Rinker said, "My wife baked some cakes last week and went out to the lake and sold them to tourists."

Beverly Beard was working at the Garrett County Welfare Board when strikers were deemed eligible for food stamps. She said, "I'm 5 feet tall. I weighed 100 pounds. They [strikers applying for welfare] were big guys. I was terrified to death. They were getting bad publicity in town. But they were nice."

"My mother supported my dad in everything," said Shari Riggleman Whetstone, daughter of striker Harold Riggleman. "I remember my mother had inherited some land on North Hill [near today's Wolf Den Run State Park]. They [father and mother] were upset but they needed to sell the land to keep some income coming in," she added.

"What a hard time we had," said Helen Fike, who went to Uniontown, Pennsylvania to redeem her food stamps, a source of help that was frowned upon in normal times. As the strike drew on and workers qualified for food stamps, union leader Hollie Atwood tried to convince them to accept the help.

"Some of the guys were reluctant to take food stamps. They were ashamed," said Doris Ray, Atwood's wife at the time. "But Hollie convinced them to take the stamps. I tried to convince him to take them, too, but he wouldn't."

"I took in sewing [during the strike]," said Mary Enlow Frazee, wife of striker Floyd Frazee, who learned the skills of a seamstress from her mother and sisters and a high school home economics class.

Troy Wakefield recalled, "The union was good to me. The union made one payment on my house and a couple smaller ones. I couldn't believe they covered my payments because I was hired only a couple months before."

Such support boosted morale. "We [teachers] supported the roads strikers. We brought them hot chocolate and pizzas and spoke with them. They were out in the cold," said Dave Beard, the charter vice-president of the Garrett County American Federation of Teachers, formed in 1968 and, later, a county commissioner.

Small businesses in town were divided on whether to support or oppose the strike. But one local couple, Harry and Louise Seggie, who owned a tavern in Accident, were given special recognition in AFSCME's *Public Employee.*

"Harry and Louise Seggie, who run Seggie's Knotty Tavern … were two of the first citizens of Garrett County to rally to the strikers' cause and Harry's Local 331 of the Utility Workers donated $500 to the strike fund."

The Seggies, who lived above the tavern, were both active in Democratic Party politics. Of Harry, his sister-in-law said, "He was a good man who always tried to help people who were down and out."

[1] Goulden, Joseph, *Jerry Wurf: Labor's Last Angry Man*, Atheneum, 1982, page 9.

14

TAKE IT TO THE BALLOT BOX

In normal times, the victors in county elections could be reasonably predicted by their support from organizational entities like the Farm Bureau or the Sheriff's Department. The unpredictable turmoil surrounding the road strike pushed aside any semblance of normalcy. The road workers and their union entered the electoral fray, strategically endorsing candidates from both parties whom they thought would settle the strike.

Elections and Final Negotiations - 1970

The Republican listed candidates for the primary election for Garrett County Board of Commissioners.

* District 1, Republican William Fitzwater challenged incumbent Allen Paugh. Democrats running included Bernard M. Guy, Mason I. Madigan and William R. Virts.
* District 2: Republicans: Charles C. Arnold, Warren E. Miller, Samuel J. Thomas, C. William Turner; Democrats: Ellis O. Cogley, Earl Opel, Allen S. Warnick.
* District 3, Republicans Arthur Savage, J. Edward Tasker and O. Dale Uphole challenged incumbent John Ross Sines. Democrats running included Wayne B. Hamilton, James E. Matthews, Asa F. Nethkin, Theodore Raynovich, and Harry Sines.

Union Picks Slates for Primary

In an open letter to former State Senator Clifford Friend, AFSCME encouraged citizens to vote for "responsible government," recommending commissioner candidates in both the Republican and Democratic primaries.

* District 1- Allen Paugh (R) and William Virts (D);
* District 2- C. William Turner (R) and Earl Opel (D)
* District 3- J. Edward Tasker (R) and Theodore Raynovich (D)

AFSCME Local 1834 President Jack Sowers also declared his candidacy for Garrett County Sheriff.

Union-Endorsed Candidate Ted Raynovich

Ted Raynovich Sr., the union's preferred candidate in District 3 (Oakland), was born into a family of Western Pennsylvania union coal miners. Raynovich worked as a union ironworker in Pittsburgh and moved to Deep Creek Lake in 1952, traveling back to Pittsburgh and other locales for work, said his son Theodore Raynovich Jr.

"My dad wasn't active in the Democratic Party," said Raynovich Jr., who worked in the Luke, Maryland paper mill and later joined his father in the ironworker trade. But, he said, his dad "went out every morning with coffee and donuts for the strikers."

It was suggested to the senior Raynovich that he run for commissioner and he did.

Raynovich Jr. said local union members held planning meetings for the campaign at his stepmother's lady's apparel store in Oakland. During the campaign, the candidate published an ad in the September 30 issue of *The Citizen* announcing a town hall meeting in Finzel. Granting recognition to road workers was at the top of his agenda.

Raynovich also advocated for more vocational schools, fighting "against pollution and polluters," winning more federal support for the county, and working with property owners on Deep Creek Lake to enhance county business.

Paugh Makes Case for Re-election

On September 12, with the primary election five days away, Commissioner Dick Paugh Sr. made his case to the voters in an interview with *The Citizen*, drawing the contrast between his service and the tenure of fellow Republicans, Sines and Friend.

Paugh outlined how, during his term on the county commission, he and fellow commissioners Earl Opel and Hub Swartzentruber had set aside $400,000 for the construction of Garrett County Community College. He said Sines and Friend had put that money back into the county budget and had cut property taxes by $.50 per $100 of value.

Paugh asserted that Sines and Friend refused to replenish money for the college until the appropriation was put to a referendum. To recoup money for the college, the commissioners were forced to float a bond issue of $315,000 that taxpayers would be paying back for 20 years at a rate of 5.25 percent.

"Sines cut property taxes looking for "election year fodder," said Paugh. In reality, the taxes could be cut only because Texas Eastern Gas Pipeline Co. was putting more money into the county's coffers, having recently lost its appeal for a reduction on its tax assessments on natural gas holdings.

Addressing the road workers' strike, Paugh said he expected the county to incur at least $100,000 in repairs necessitated by the county's failure to keep up with regular maintenance during the strike. He pointed out that two county roads engineers [DeWitt and Sluss] had quit since the strike began.

Concluding his broadside, Paugh said Sines and Friend had enabled a private firm, Mellott Co., to take significant tonnage of rock from the face of the county's quarry with no public approval. And his fellow commissioners had paid thousands of dollars to road workers who either refused to strike or were newly hired but performed no work.

Sines and Paugh Defeated in Huge Turnout

On September 15, *The Citizen* reported that Garrett County's 52 percent turnout in the primary election was the highest in the nation, another record set amidst the nation's longest public worker strike.

Sines lost his nomination to J. Edward Tasker by 175 votes out of 2,401 total ballots. Paugh lost to William Fitzwater by 161 votes out of 2,993 total ballots. Ross Sines had made good on his promise to deny Paugh another term.

Voters nominated William Fitzwater (R) and Bernard Guy (D) in District 1, Samuel J. Thomas (R) and Earl Opel (D) in District 2, and Edward Tasker (R) and Wayne Hamilton (D) in District 3.

In a *Citizen* editorial, Rosenbaum wrote: "First-comers to politics can chalk up their large votes to just one thing: the union's help."

While only two of the union's recommended candidates, J. Edward Tasker (R) and Earl Opel (D) won their races, the paper said the high vote totals for the union-endorsed candidates running against the [political] "machines" reflected its influence.

The newspaper asked voters to "pay attention" during the upcoming campaign, warning that Republican candidate Sam Thomas had "supported the scabs and had a county payloader, [a piece of heavy equipment outfitted with a scoop to move dirt and gravel], "conveniently parked" in his barn.

Rosenbaum labeled William Fitzwater from district 1 a "hay-pitching friend" of defeated Commissioner Sines. Tasker, the Republican who defeated Sines, told newspapers he had "nothing to do with the union's endorsement."

AFSCME Local 1834 President Jack Sowers lost his primary challenge to fellow Democrat J.F. Browning.

"I Wanted to Show the Union I Wasn't Afraid."

"I felt like a weight had been lifted off my back [after losing]," said Sines. "I had only made $4,500 a year. I tried to serve my time on the county well." He recalled the days when he put a clutch in a county truck, plowed snow or traveled to Glen Burnie just south of Baltimore to pick up a blacktopping machine.

He took pride in the "50 miles of blacktop a year" the machine produced. "Some of my work was appreciated. Some wasn't," said Sines, who remembered one of his former schoolteachers telling him that running for commissioner put him in contention for "one of the most unthankful jobs you could have taken on."

Sines had refused to campaign in the primary. At many different junctures of the strike, he had envisioned the tide of public disapproval sinking the union's standing and widening support for his refusal to recognize AFSCME. He was wrong.

Sines held from the start that many strikers were disaffected from the union and ready to go back to work. He believed most of the ministers who signed the letter offering to mediate the dispute were on his side, only to be manipulated by the union coal miner, Rev. George Tichinel.

After the violent confrontation on the parking lot, he anticipated that the union, not he and Friend, would be blamed for weeks of stalemated talks, the worsening of the roads and the violence against property. He had joined preacher Homer Mellott passing out Bible tracts during the bus battle and expected strikers to be the ones punished for their defiance, not himself and Friend.

Instead, Sines and Friend had alienated nearly the entire established order of the county, from sheriffs with families on the picket line, to State Police officers and even Judge Hamill, the Democrat who had declared the strike illegal.

Any notion that a Democratic governor would call out the National Guard to bust a union in a Republican county at the request of two adversaries only showed Sines' and Friends' detachment from political reality.

Sines said he felt betrayed by road workers, especially by those for whom he had done favors and stretched the rules, but who nevertheless struck. He criticized *The Republican* for supporting "everything liberal" during the strike, even though the paper had lobbed its sharpest darts at the union.

He and his fellow commissioners had accomplished much during their term. But in the end, Sines' entrenched grudge proved to be his downfall.

"I ran [in the primary] because I wanted to know how many

friends I had left and to show the union I wasn't afraid of them. And I wanted to take Dick Paugh with me [to defeat]," said Sines.

"We had television coverage of the strike and the Lord was 'working on the strikers,'" he added. "The strike was caused by a problem [Paugh] right at our desk. Everyone knew he couldn't be trusted."

Paugh told *The Sun:* "This is a great burden off my shoulders. Now I can come to my farm and live happily ever after, fillin' silos."

The General Election Campaign

Homer L. Bennett, chairman of the Garrett County Republican Central Committee and a member of the influential Naylor family, now knew Republicans were being decisively blamed for the strike.

Bennett appealed to tradition and party loyalty to prevent an unprecedented Democratic rout on Election Day. His first tug came in the October 15 issue of *The Republican* in a paid ad headlined: "Points to Ponder in the Upcoming General Election."

"We are fortunate not to have many of their [Democrats'] downstate city problems," wrote Bennett, listing "overcrowding, civil disorders, high taxation, pollution, sewage disposal, uncontrolled industrial expansion, extensive drug abuse and soaring crime rates."

The downstate reference to civil disorders was transparent to county residents who were watching the national news or communicating with their relatives in Baltimore.

On April 21, 1970, a white policeman was killed in Baltimore. A member of the Black Panther Party was charged with the murder. A week later, 150 Baltimore City Police officers raided the Panther's headquarters on Aisquith St. in East Baltimore.

Bennett made no mention of unions, the year's wave of national strikes, or, most tellingly, the labor confrontation that was still consuming Garrett County. Under the axiom "all politics is local," Bennett would have to acknowledge his party's role in the chaos.

Instead, he made light of the party's failure, concluding, "We have our growing pains and problems to be sure and there are some people who will point out that a change in the administration is a sure, quick answer for [the] county's ills, both real and imagined.

"But the best way to solve our problems is through careful and responsible planning and controlled, steady growth. And that's the type of leadership Republican administrations have always shown."

During their primary campaigns, Democratic candidates Hamilton, Opel and Guy had worked to project an image of competence and stability. In the general election campaign, they seized the opportunity to claim the mantle of calm and progress.

The message: You blew it up. We can put it back together.

Wayne Hamilton, a farmer from Red House at the southern end of the county, listed his education at the top of his political ad, touting his graduation from the University of Maryland in 1936.

Next he featured 20 years of business experience as a dairy farmer and his religious affiliation, Church of the Brethren.

Finally, he touted his organizational memberships: 25 years in the Farm Bureau, serving as its legislative chairman, vice president of the Garrett County Development Corporation.

Bernard Guy, from Bloomington, bordering Allegany County and the Luke paper mill, promoted his business acumen as a builder and insurance agent, and his service in WWII. Like Hamilton, he listed his membership in the Farm Bureau and the Garrett County Development Corporation.

Guy called upon voters to "Put men with business experience and common sense in office to administer our county business."

Earl Opel was the owner of a successful fruit and vegetable market on Long Stretch, a section of the historic National Road at the county's northeastern end. He reminded voters of his four years of service on the commission from 1962 to 1966, marked by "sensible, progressive county government."

Opel said, "The economic structure of our County has been damaged by those who are only concerned with a grudge or a 'get-even' policy. Certainly this is no prospectus for our future."

The road workers' strike, said Opel, "is our major problem at hand and in my opinion, can be handled feasibly and legally in all aspects. I have negotiated with these men before and can do so again. Let us not forget they are the basic backbone of our entire economic structure in the County."

Commissioner Resignations Sought

On Sept. 3, Homer Bennett and the county's Republican central committee — in discussions with commissioners — considered a plan to settle the strike before the upcoming election. The plan would entail the resignations of Friend, Sines and Paugh and appointing three interim commissioners.

Maryland State law provides that the majority party in a county fills vacancies upon approval of the governor. Bennett submitted a list of more than a dozen names to commissioners who would, in turn, select the three interim members.

The Republican reported Governor Mandel was planning to head to Garrett County to discuss the interim plan on the radio but was delayed because of "drug problems" in Baltimore. Two days before, Baltimore was part of a three-state raid on a suspected drug dealing operation.

It was rumored the governor would seek to certify the newly-elected commissioners as soon as possible *after* the November 4 election to smooth the path toward a strike settlement. Normally, new commissioners were not certified in election years until sometime around Dec. 1.

Hamill Takes Strike to Grand Jury

On September 16, with the union's contempt hearing postponed, Judge Stuart F. Hamill II convened a grand jury to consider his proposal to settle the strike. Hamill told the *Baltimore Sun* the stalemated lockout was "deplorable" and said he wanted to see the road workers back on the job to launch a "crash road repair" program before winter.

Hamill's proposal was similar to a plan forwarded by *The Republican*. He called for 50 striking road workers to return to work immediately, followed closely by 50 more. He further proposed that a union representation election, under a federal mediator, take place no more than 60 days after road workers' return to work.

The workers would have the right to join AFSCME. The

commissioners would then be able to "exercise their responsibility for road repairs." Any disputes could be settled in arbitration. Hamill gave the grand jury the option of "considering or ignoring" his suggestions.

On September 17, *The Baltimore Sun* reported that Commissioner Friend was still considering Hamill's suggestion to submit the road worker dispute to mediation. On September 22, 100 road workers met at American Legion in Oakland and voted not to return to work. Five men chose to retire rather than remain on the picket lines.

State Comptroller Denies Tax Relief

On September 24, Maryland State Comptroller Louis Goldstein responded to Virginia Rosenbaum's request for tax abatements covering Garrett County residents since the county had stopped repairing roads. He said no relief could be granted. Goldstein said state funds for county roads are derived from gasoline taxes and are "independent of whether county commissioners have legal responsibility for maintaining roads."

Answering speculation that the state roads department would take responsibility for plowing Garrett County's roads if the strike was not settled, John Bushby, the state's District 6 engineer, said his crew of 60 men "could not possibly handle the county workload."

On October 8, the *Cumberland New*s reported that Virginia Rosenbaum was calling for Garrett County residents who owned snowmobiles to form a "snowmobile brigade" that could serve residents "should an emergency arrive," while roads were unplowed.

AFSCME Proposes Settlement

AFSCME Special Representative Alva Lewis published a paid letter in *The Republican* on Sept. 24. declaring that road workers and their representatives have "always been and are still willing to negotiate this dispute." Lewis listed the terms of a temporary settlement that could be initiated with commission candidates that might win election in November.

      *   The county would recognize Local 1834.

* Dues check-off would be initiated upon their return to work or no later than Jan. 1971.
* No reprisals against road workers who belong to the union with reinstatement to their former positions.
* Road workers would receive the same wages and fringe benefits already offered to strikebreakers.
* Negotiations would begin with the new commissioners no later than 30 days after they were sworn into office with all the above provisions to remain in force until a new contract was negotiated.

Lewis ended his letter stating: "None of the above precludes our negotiating with the present County Commissioners immediately if they will agree to do so."

Residents Propose Referendum on Recognition

On October 13, a group of residents suggested that county recognition of Local 1834 be put to a referendum on the November 3 ballot. The group proposing the referendum included: Martin Friend, Clarence Deal, Glen Keller, R. Dale Fike, Mr. and Mrs. Mitchell Rush, D.T. Rush, Ralph Hoye, Brison Thomas, F. Savage, and Jim Bowman.

The proposal was described in the commission's minutes: "The question should be worded so that the referendum would not be acceptance or rejection of the Union for workers but would serve as a guide as to the general feeling of County Voters concerning recognition of the Union for County Employees."

The commissioners discussed with State's Attorney Fred A. Thayer the legal questions surrounding a referendum being initiated so close to an election. Thayer speculated that the referendum could pass legal muster only if it was "informational." Sines moved for approval of a referendum. His fellow commissioners gave unanimous support.

The minutes concluded: "It was felt that such information would be of great value to the new Board in dealing with the Roads problem…The suggestion was made [by the visiting group] that all people requesting employment with the County be given written and physical examinations. It also was suggested that striking road workers be barred from picketing [on] County Property."

Had the issue of union recognition gone to referendum, would the voters have kept it separate from the mass firing of their neighbors and family members and the deteriorating condition of the roads? Or would large numbers of voters agree with Oakland resident Jasper Riley, who showed up at a commission meeting on October 13?

Riley said he "was not in favor of the union as such." But he said he felt the recognition of the union "would have come" anyway, and the board should have yielded to that inevitability and avoided the strike, the chaos, and the disruption of road maintenance.

The Republican to Workers: "Give a Little"

In an October 15 editorial, *The Republican* stated: "If the road workers don't give a little, they will be charged as being just as bullheaded, contrary and unreasonable as they have consistently charged the two commissioners, really more so since there are so many more of them."

The newspaper called upon road workers to be "civic minded as they were last winter [forestalling their strike]" and go back to work, renewing negotiations with the new commissioners once they take office.

Interim Commission Plan Delayed

On October 22, Republican Chairman Homer Bennett announced the party's selections of interim commissioners: Dr. Ralph Calandrella, a general practitioner from Kitzmiller; Tom Butscher, owner of WKMG Radio in Oakland; and Ross Selby, a timberman from Friendsville.

According to *The Citizen*, the interim commissioners had already quickly negotiated a tentative agreement with the union. But Chairman Bennett and *The Citizen* were blindsided. *The Republican* reported that

Sines, Friend and Paugh had all delayed their resignations.

Republicans: "Don't Change Habits"

With the strike still unsettled, Homer Bennett made his last plea to voters in an October 22 ad in *The Republican.* "Don't be too quick to change the voting habits of a lifetime. Most of us in Garrett County are Republicans, and most of us have voted the straight Republican ticket more often than not."

Young voters were pressured to tow the party line. One of the roads strikers recalled how deeply party affiliation was pushed within families. Returning home to Garrett County after his military service, he had registered to vote. After the mail arrived from the board of elections, he remembered his grandmother approaching him, saying: "I can't believe what you did. You registered as a Democrat. I don't know what to think of you anymore."

Interim Plan Fails

On October 29, Friend, Paugh and Sines resigned. According to the *Baltimore Sun,* the resignations came at the urging of Thomas Butscher, the Oakland radio station manager and one of three interim commissioners appointed by the Republican Central Committee.

With the election only a few days away, Democratic Del. B.O. Aiken asked Governor Mandel to pull back from approving the interim commission.

The Citizen stated: "The Governor legally has 15 days before he must appoint [interim commissioners], and because he is 'playing politics' along with a few others in Garrett County who have contacted him, he is taking his legal time to hold off the appointments until after the election."

Mandel was playing with a winning hand. He refused to cut a deal to enable his Republican adversaries to take credit, for settling the strike just before an election. Sines and Friend had ignited the conflict; they and their party needed to pay the political price.

The *Washington Post* reported that a spokesman for the governor said the appointments of the interim commissioners were delayed because "no letters of resignation from the former commissioners had been forwarded to Annapolis and because a Republican county leader charged that the nominations were made illegally."

Whatever the circumstances, Democrats were now playing the political hand given them by their adversaries, leaving the responsibility for the strike on Republican strategists.

Sines, now a lame duck, told *The Republican* he had desired a referendum on union recognition, as requested by some residents, but "time had run out." But time had not run out. The coming election would, in fact, now be that referendum.

15

THE PEOPLE HAVE SPOKEN

"You have got to unite in the same labor union and in the same political party and strike and vote together, and the hour you do that, the world is yours."
                                                                    - Eugene V. Debs / 1855-1926

Three Democrats Win Commission in 67% Turnout

The Citizen's Nov. 5 headline read: "First Time in History—Garrett Goes Demo." Democrat Bernard Guy defeated Republican William Fitzwater in District 1 by a vote of 3,321 to 2,409. Democrat Earl Opel of Long Stretch in District 2 defeated Republican Sam Thomas 3,731 votes to 1,996. And Democrat Wayne Hamilton defeated Republican J. Edward Tasker in District 3,579 to 2,181.

The Citizen reported: "This blows to pieces several Garrett County myths ... One, the people don't like Unions, and two, the people vote Republican regardless. It just isn't true!"

Wendell Beitzel, a Garrett County native who later served as Republican county commissioner and a member of the House of Delegates, was working in Washington, D.C. as a microbiologist at the National Institutes of Health during the strike.

"I was up there [Garrett County] every weekend and followed the strike," said Beitzel. "I knew Friend and Sines and I knew Dick Paugh real well."

"It can't be overstated," said Beitzel, "how positive Dick Paugh's impact was in Garrett County," referencing Paugh's support for Garrett College. "Paugh would have been re-elected and Wayne Hamilton and the Democrats would never have been elected if Sines and Friend weren't so bullheaded and had settled the strike."

The Republican reported that 67 percent of eligible voters showed up at the polls, despite "rainy, foggy weather," with some precincts reporting up to 75 percent turnout. While Democrats won an unprecedented victory on the Garrett County Board of Commissioners, leading members of the party were defeated elsewhere.

B.O. Aiken lost his delegate seat spanning Garrett County and parts of Allegany County, finishing 858 votes behind Republican DeCoursey Bolden. Rev. W.H. Leake of the right-wing American Party received 866 votes. Governor Mandel won re-election. But Republican J. Glenn Beall Jr. of Cumberland overwhelmed Senator Joseph Tydings.

The Citizen reported, "[Tydings] incurred the wrath of the general public and the powerful gun companies when he brought forth legislation for gun registration."

During his campaign, Beall linked Tydings to a list of problems that Beall claimed were symptomatic of Democratic governance: "Marylanders are fed up with bombings, campus violence, riots, experimentation in education, shooting of policemen, tax dollar waste, the drug culture—the whole permissive mess."

The political pendulum in Western Maryland even more strongly favored Republicans. Only the roads strike kept Garrett County's commission race from swinging in the same direction.

Tentative Agreement Signed

On November 12, the newly-elected commissioners asked the lame duck commissioners for authorization to negotiate with the union. Their request was denied. With their swearing in expected to take place on November 17 (earlier than past commissions), Hamilton, Opel and Guy defied the interim appointees and met with AFSCME Local 1834 leaders.

On November 17, less than 20 minutes after their swearing in, the new commissioners signed a tentative agreement with AFSCME Local 1834. The union was represented by Local 1834 President Jack Sowers, Ernest Crofoot, Alva Lewis, and Michael Lindner.

AFSCME Local 1834 members ratified the agreement at a meeting at 8 p.m. *The Citizen* published the entire pact on its

November 19 front page. Terms of agreement included a secret ballot representation election by road workers within three days, supervised by Alva Lewis for the union, Jack Turney, the newly appointed Garrett County Attorney, and impartial member Gerald Minnich.

The new commissioners promised to recognize AFSCME Local 1834 if road workers voted in favor of representation. To qualify to vote on whether to approve AFSCME's tentative contract, workers were required to be available for work or to renew their employment by the Garrett County Roads Department. To do so they had to leave outside jobs they'd taken during the strike.

The agreement contained the following provisions:

* No reprisals against any employee who participated in the strike; no coercion or reprisals against any of the workers who *did not* strike or against any new workers hired during the strike.
* Full seniority to be returned to workers who struck, providing they report to work within 15 days.
* Dues check-off for all employees who authorized such deductions (authorization could be canceled upon 30 days' notice).
* Wage increases and fringe benefits enumerated in the County Commissioners' budget, paid as of the workers' return to work.
* Immediate negotiations to reach a full agreement in 60 days.
* Work in excess of eight hours in any 24-hour period, or in excess of 40 hours in any one week would be compensated at time and one-half "based on an ability [of the county] to pay".
* Any employee could join any organization he shall elect, "other than those which would be subversive to any local, state or national government.
* Membership in any organization, association, union, or federation would not be a condition of employment.

The last point was critical. To gain recognition and conclude a first agreement, the union had given up requiring an "agency shop." Union membership in Garrett County would be voluntary, unlike other AFSCME units where the union contract made union membership a condition of employment.

The agreement specified that it covered *only* the Garrett County Roads Department and "excludes all other Garrett County Departments or organizations."

The settlement was widely covered in the local, national, and labor press. AFSCME's *The Public Employee* interviewed Local 1834 President Jack Sowers, who noted, "not one piece of machinery moved [during the strike] and not one man crossed a picket line."

AFSCME International President Wurf told his paper: "It [roads strike] is one of the most remarkable demonstrations of solidarity and determination that we have ever seen in the union. And that is what won the strike.

"The men of Local 1834 have given Garrett County an education in unionism. They've made it clear that they won't be pushed around by the boss. They have demanded and won a measure of dignity on the job and the hope of a better life for their families."

Recalling the threats his wife and others received during the battle, Sowers said, "It may take a year or so for people to get over their bitterness about this strike, but I believe they eventually will."

Sowers added that his local was already preparing for the upcoming negotiations. He told *The Public Employee*: "...we are ready to go out again for eight months if we had to."

The *Baltimore Sun* wrote: "The settlement was announced with little fanfare about 5:30 p.m. in the County Courthouse...[in] the conservative, mountainous region...with contract negotiations to begin within 60 days, the road workers will be bargaining in mid-January from a strong position..."

Commenting on the shape of the roads, *The Sun* noted, "...Motorists are forced to slalom around literally thousands of deep, jagged potholes that will become even more dangerous when covered with a blanket of snow."

John Murphy, a storeowner, told *The Sun*: "The county roads are in such bad shape that if we had a heavy snow, the farmers could not get their milk to market, and business in town would be pretty much shot."

The Republican reported that crews left the garages for work within two hours of the union vote and were already repairing dirt roads and putting up snow fences. Some road workers continued to picket the county garages after the settlement until they returned to work.

The Sun wrote: "A young road worker said the continuance of the picket lines was to 'show the public that we mean business and that we will stick together.'"

AFSCME Local 1834 leader Leo Rinker told the *Sun*: "Unionism is a dirty word in Garrett County, but it looks like the people in the county have to live with it now."

On November 19, *The Republican* reported that, out of 141 eligible to vote, road workers had opted 119 to 10, to affiliate with AFSCME. The ballots were counted by County Attorney Jack Turney, AFSCME leader Alva Lewis and neutral observer Gerald Minnich, a local funeral home owner.

Since the strike began, two road workers had died, one had resigned and several had found other jobs.

The Republican reported the roads department tried but failed to continue its contract with Phoenix Construction Co., the firm that was making hot-mix asphalt to fill potholes. Instead, the county contracted with "a company in Springs, Pa." to supply cold mix asphalt to begin filling potholes.

Acting roads engineer Clayton Smith told the newspaper it would take nearly a year for the roads to return to normal condition.

On November 26, *The Citizen* published its inaugural *Commissioners' News* column. Opel, Hamilton, and Guy reported that roads department equipment was in "exceptionally good shape" with "no damage done to the extent of all the rumors going around."

Many people, they said, "stopped by to compliment the County Commissioners in regard to their quick settlement of the road department situation."

Roads Engineer Paul W. DeWitt Rehired

On November 30, the commissioners rehired Paul W. DeWitt as administrative engineer of the Garrett County Roads Department. DeWitt had served in that capacity for 12 years before the strike.

Former Garrett County Administrator Marshall Rickert, who arrived in the county after the strike, said, "Paul DeWitt was involved in many things beyond the roads department as a senior resource person. He was a good soul, a friend, a healer." The commissioners commended Clayton Smith, who had worked as acting engineer during the strike.

The new commissioners introduced a "new and more sophisticated [application] form for employment." On December 8, a day designated as "Road Board Day," 100 applicants were reviewed for re-employment on the county roads. One day later, formal contract negotiations began between AFSCME Local 1834 and the Garrett County Board of Commissioners. On December 10, Martha Glotfelty, administrative secretary of the roads department, an outspoken critic of the union, resigned.

One week later, Administrative Engineer DeWitt met with Democratic U.S. Rep. Goodloe Byron. He presented plans to re-implement the state and federal assistance for new roads in Garrett County. DeWitt told Byron that $800,000 had been "programmed for new roads" but was not "taken advantage of by the former board [commissioners]."

An all-day negotiation session was held on January 7, 1971, between AFSCME and the county. Present were the county commissioners, Paul DeWitt, Jack Turney, assisted by George Farmer, a Morgantown, West Virginia attorney, and Ernie Crofoot and Alva Lewis on behalf of the union. The next meeting was scheduled for Jan 15. The meeting was contentious and led to talk about another strike.

New Strike Threat

On January 15, Peter Morales, from AFSCME Baltimore Council 67, sent a memo to P.J. Ciampa at the union's international headquarters. "I have been informed by Director Crofoot that there are serious problems in Garrett County. The new County Commissioner hired a 'union busting' attorney [George Farmer] from West Virginia and has submitted the enclosed Memorandum of Accord.

"Please note on the last page they are requesting the International President and an International Representative to sign the agreement. A strike deadline has been set for Monday, January 18, 1971. The Council Representatives are in Garrett County now trying to resolve this explosive situation."

The "explosive situation" was quickly averted. The commissioners and Local 1834 met on January 16. The commission minutes stated the meeting began at 2 p.m. and ended at 1 a.m. when a "working agreement" was reached.

The January 18 commission minutes state the agreement was "virtually the same as the last Garrett County Roads Employees' Association agreement," incorporating the back-to-work language, a more definitive grievance procedure, plus a 5-percent wage increase. It covered all county roads employees except those employees classified as administrative, clerical, technical, professional and area supervisors. Union members ratified the contract on January 18 by a vote of 103 to 3.

The memo sent by Peter Morales on January 15 to P. J. Ciampa, warning of a strike, was marked "Settled 1/17/71."

16

THE AFTERMATH

"But to look back from the stony plain along the road which led one to that place is not at all the same thing as walking on the road; the perspective to say the very least, changes only with the journey; only when the road has, all abruptly and treacherously, and with an absoluteness that permits no argument, turned or dropped or risen is one able to see all that one could not have seen from any other place."

- James Baldwin, *Go Tell It on the Mountain*

After the battle of the bus, Ross Sines called Governor Mandel and warned him there would be bloodshed in the county if Mandel didn't supply more police or National Guard intervention. Local 1834 President Jack Sowers had said they would go to "knuckle junction" or worse if strikebreakers were brought through the picket lines. *The Citizen* and *The Republican* echoed the forecasts of violence.

Strikers and their opponents had sustained no injuries. Hubert Friend, the gentle farmer, and Ross Sines, deemed to be the most "stubborn," "hard-headed" man in the county, never surrendered. But they had made good on their solemn promise to avoid violence by not mounting another effort to bring strikebreakers through the picket lines.

At least one of the residents accompanying Sines to defend the bus on August 15 was armed. The union folks carried clubs. But Sines, in the manner of Church of the Brethren pacifism, passed out Bible tracts amidst the tension. Sines had avoided violence, but he wasn't inclined to forgive or forget.

"I'd see strikers in church [after the settlement]," said Sines. "I'd say, 'Striker, how are you doing today?'" Sines reserved his sharpest words for those he felt betrayed him.

"You'll be a striker [to me] until they put you in the casket," Sines told road worker Joe Whitacre. He hadn't moderated fifty years later, saying. "A man should keep his word."

Sines also singled out Asa Wilhelm for disloyalty. Sines said Wilhelm, the savvy Republican political leader in Finzel, whose picnics had always been obligatory for office seekers, told Sines during his re-election campaign, "There are many reasons why we should vote for Ross Sines."

After that discussion, Wilhelm supported the Democrats, including Earl Opel, who was married to Wilhelm's niece. Asa Wilhelm's son Allen said, "My dad told me the only way to resolve [the roads strike] would be [with] a new board of commissioners."

Asa Wilhelm's iconoclasm was honed years before. Along with a group of farmers in the Finzel area, he had protested sending their children to the new Northern High School built in the early 1950's, contending that the 50-minute round trip to Accident each day would undermine the youths' labor on their family farms.

"Dad and the farmers asked for a meeting with George Edwards of the board of education," said Allen Wilhelm. They told Edwards, 'We can't live with this.'" Wilhelm said Edwards told the farmers, 'You'll probably be prosecuted' [for truancy]. The farmers held out and, in 1952, Garrett County negotiated an agreement to allow students in the area to attend nearby Beall High School and elementary schools in Allegany County.

For years after his election loss, Sines showed up periodically at public meetings, mostly to argue against growing the county's spending. In the late 70s, Sines testified in a hearing opposing county support for a new wing at Garrett County Memorial Hospital.

"Ross had a right to his own ways," said former commissioner Ernie Gregg, "But I remember Sines making an anti-Semitic slur against three of the hospital administrators who had Jewish backgrounds and were speaking in support of the new wing. That was wrong."

In 2019, Sines—who periodically traveled to Baltimore to pass out Bible tracts at predominantly Black high schools—said the strike and AFSCME's arrival were just more evidence of a still-developing apocalypse.

181

"I'm not here to lift myself up, but to lift up the Lord, Jesus Christ," said Sines. "America doesn't have anything to be proud of. We took the land from the Indians. We brought Black people here to work.

"Politicians have done things they shouldn't and it's going to get a lot worse. Rightly so, you will have rebellions and America will someday have a famine … for dumping meat and 'taters' in the ocean to keep prices up."

He prayed for then-President Donald Trump's success in defeating liberalism, while acknowledging his concerns over the president's moral failings.

No apocalypse was evident in the county garages after the strike. Perhaps the most remarkable feature of the strike was the tolerant climate after the months of conflict ended.

When it was over, it was over. Strikers went to work beside strikebreakers who had continued to collect paychecks during the strike. There were no serious confrontations between them. Non-retaliation was one of the conditions of the strike settlement. But it seems the lack of a grudge match was more attributable to the county's culture than any legal mandate.

The ending of the road strike lacked the acrimony and bitterness reported after confrontations in coal mining towns across Appalachia. It was probably easier for strikers to forgive elected commissioners who were, after all, still neighbors down the road, than for miners and their families to forgive wealthy, far-flung capitalists or the local politicians who did their bidding. Despite their intransigence, Sines and Friend had not risked more confrontations between strikers and their adversaries after the battle of the bus.

Perhaps the unity built over eight months gave the strikers the confidence to simply move on, knowing they were in the strong majority. Maybe, like in the case of strikebreaker Owen Bach, the Battle of the Bulge veteran who was a leader of the roads employees' association but refused to strike, AFSCME members took a "live and let live" approach to those who opposed the union.

Terry Rinker, Leo's son, grew up alongside the children of Accident resident Owen Bach. "I know that there were some hard feelings between my dad and Bach [over the strike] and words were

182

spoken, but as far as I know there was never anything retaliatory done," he said.

The short window between the end of the conflict and the coming of the snows left no trifling time for a union that had banked on public support by deliberately delaying their strike until after the prior winter. The unity of the picket line now needed to be redirected to filling potholes, grading, erecting snow fences, plowing roads, making blacktop, and building bridges.

Donna Evans, the wife of striker Rodger Evans, said, "People were happy to get back to work. We kept on going. That's what I'm thankful for, that it ended the way it did. I think the guys that are working there [at the garages] now should be thankful for what they have."

"After a while, everybody got along. Seems like nobody held a grudge," said Jim Fike. His wife, Helen, added, "It [the strike] is not something we're real proud of. Not everybody wants to say anything about it. I think we got very little extra money. But we got recognized that we were a union. We never bothered anybody that didn't ask to be bothered."

"We're all children of God. Bitterness doesn't get you anywhere," said Mary Frazee, wife of striker Floyd Frazee.

Bryan Sines, the strikebreaker hired by Ross Sines who reportedly asked if he could handle a gun, was hired after the strike and worked 17 years on the county roads. He never joined the union, according to his his wife, Lillian Sines. But, she said, he was "popular with the men" who gave him a hunting rifle upon his retirement.

Harold Riggleman served on the county's Democratic Central Committee and was promoted to foreman after the strike, said his daughter, Shari Riggleman Whetstone, who worked at Bausch and Lomb and Verso's Westvaco Paper mill before it shut down in 2019.

"Everything went back to natural after the strike," said Sheldon Whitacre. His wife, Nadean Whitacre said, "The county [leaders] were just too old-fashioned and didn't want to change."

Ross Sines, she said, was "set in his ways," but she added, "I was set in my ways, too. Like the old country song says, 'You gotta stand for something or you'll fall for anything.'"

Nadean Whitacre, who was baptized by Jonas Sines, Ross Sines' father, and remembers Jonas Sines joining dinners at her home, said, "I can't hold anything against Ross. He stood up for what he believed in."

Asked to explain the lack of conflict after the strike and the county historical society's absence of documentation of the conflict, Leo Miller said, "Garrett County is a laid-back place. People keep their thoughts to themselves. We were raised that way. I think the strike was good for the county. It kind of had an uplifting effect on wages and building. But [after the strike] everything was swept under the rug, and we went about our business."

Miller's description of the county's sense of privacy was underscored by a striker's widow, who in 2020, brought out one of her husband's pay stubs from the 1950s, but cautioned that, "if they're made public," his name should be blacked out because "he wouldn't want everyone to know [how much he was paid]."

Two widows of strikers talked about brothers-in-law who were would-be scabs, paid by the county, while refusing to join the strike. One of the widows said, "I could have wrung peoples' necks who crossed the picket line, like my brother-in-law. He was the scum of the earth, taking food out of our mouths."

Despite their bitterness, both asked that the names of the strikebreaking relatives not be revealed.

✿✿✿

Poor families don't usually have much to fight over when a member dies. But affluence can fuel conflict. Many strikers said the most notable conflicts in the county as the strike died down weren't between financially strapped workers who fell out on different sides of the roads strike. Instead, the county's legendary rivalries were between some of the wealthy local businessmen like the Brownings and the Naylors, who contended over land, property, money, and influence.

With the end of the strike, the local union now needed to be consolidated, a single bargaining unit of a much larger organization with a mission more all-encompassing than the road workers' association that preceded it. Conflicts over the union's priorities and functioning were inevitable. Like soldiers distanced from the heat of battle, the returning road workers now had more time to assess the strengths and weaknesses of their leaders, their fellow combatants, and their units.

"Unions are good if they do it right," said a striker who remained anonymous. But he said some of his co-workers "hid behind the union," looking for cover for poor attendance or not properly performing their jobs. He blamed the "guys [union leaders] from Baltimore coming in and hiring whomever they wanted as union representatives."

Paul Cosner, who had spent a year in prison for dynamiting Commissioner Friend's fence, said he needed help from the union to pay for a furnace that had failed during his time in prison, but didn't get it.

"If I had it to do all over again, I wouldn't have gone on strike," said Cosner, who apologized to Friend upon his release.

After the settlement, several of the foremen lobbied to remain in the union. A compromise was struck with some of the newly-appointed foremen staying in the union ranks and some, including Local 1834's former president, Jack Sowers, remaining outside the bargaining unit.

Ernest Friend, one of the union's leaders, who ran the crusher at the Sang Run quarry, was promoted to foreman. When the quarry shut down, he was transferred to the Oakland garage. But Friend told his sons he was uncomfortable being an "office man."

Sheldon Whitacre began supervising a paving crew. Three years after the strike, Leo Miller became a foreman in the Grantsville garage. Jim Fike supervised the bridge building crew. Johnny Tasker, the supervisor who chose to join his fellow workers on the picket line, rather than continuing to work and be paid as a strikebreaker, returned to supervision of the blacktop crew after the settlement.

"I am proud that we went out [on strike]," said Tasker in 2019. "I felt we were in the right. If I didn't think we were in the right, I would have walked away. If it wasn't for Friend and Sines, the strike wouldn't have lasted two days."

Asked what he won by going on strike, Tasker said, "Respect."

Miller, Tasker, and Whitacre said they took pride in their roles as supervisors. "I had a standard and everybody knew it," said Miller. "If I had a problem [with one of the men], I resolved it and didn't bring it back up the next day. I knew everyone who worked for me. I was responsible for a crew of 42 and 250 miles of road."

Tasker recalled helping a truck driver working outside of his area of responsibility who was having trouble handling his snowplow. Tasker said another supervisor told him he didn't know anyone else who "would do what you do," adding that his immediate supervisor told him, "You look out for your men too much."

After the settlement, many of the strikers' sons followed their fathers into the roads department. Tom Holler, son of striker Lyden "Roy" Holler, a foreman in the Oakland garage, went to work on the roads in 1971. He started out as a laborer, ran power saws and trucks and was a part-time foreman before retiring in 2007.

"The county really came a long way [with the union]," said Holler in 2020. "The younger road workers don't understand what it was before. They are giving up stuff for nothing. It could happen again that they work for nothing and will be sent home without protection. I'll take a union any day over not having it."

John Nazelrod, whose father Eugene and three uncles worked on the roads, was hired in 1971, two years after returning from service in Vietnam. "My dad and uncles said, 'You don't want to go to work there,'" said Nazelrod, a distant cousin of Commissioner Dick Paugh. "But all you had was Sterling Processing (chicken plant) or [working for] the state."

Nazelrod worked for the roads for a few years and left to work on construction. But he said he appreciated the fight his family waged. "The union members [today] need to realize just what it took to get the union. They need to keep the union alive and strong or it won't last."

Lonnie Artice, the son of striker Ray Artice, went to work on the county roads in 1980 after being advised by his doctor to leave his job at Wenzel Boat Co., where he was suffering breathing problems from fiberglass exposure. Artice retired as a truck driver and foreman on the roads. In a 2019 interview, he said: "The young guys don't realize that, without a union, they wouldn't have their wages. For the longest time the county road workers even had some better benefits than state highway workers."

Jeff Friend, the son of striker Ernest Friend, went to work on the roads in 1977 after serving in the U.S. Air Force's North American Aerospace Defense Command (NORAD). He was later elected president of Local 1834.

"The union [in the roads department] changed things. We [had been] lepers," said Friend, who was later promoted to supervisor and retired from the county's solid waste department in 2015. "Now road workers are making $27 an hour. The union raised all wages."

Ed Filsinger, the son of John Filsinger, a founder of the road workers association, was hired on the county roads in 1978, starting as a night shift mechanic, later working as a truck driver and sign shop technician. Filsinger, who learned mechanical work beside his father repairing farm equipment and cars, retired in 2006.

Allen Fike, the son of Helen and John Fike, followed his father onto the bridge crew in 1978. He retired in 2018. Fike and his siblings took his parents on vacations to Alaska, Hawaii, Newfoundland, and on hunting trips out West.

"We used to think it was a big thing just to go to Uniontown [Pennsylvania]," said Helen Fike, praising the prosperity enjoyed by road workers in the decades since the county's recognition of the union.

Wayne Miller, Leo's son, was hired by the county roads in 1977 and retired from the Grantsville garage in 2010. In 2025, his wife, Theresa Miller, was still working as the administrative roads' coordinator for the Garrett County Department of Public Works.

Respect for Local 1834 and the families who fought for recognition in 1970 ran into upper management ranks. Jeff DeWitt, parts manager at the Oakland garage, was a union member for 17 years and had uncles who worked on the roads. When materials were being moved from the former Oakland garage on Rte. 219 to the current location on Md. Rte. 135, DeWitt found a dust-covered wooden picket sign from the strike. He cleaned it up and union members set it atop a bank of lockers in the garage's locker room.

Victor Nazelrod Jr., the son and nephew of strikers, recalled forming friendships with the children of strike leader Tom Spiker and other road workers at rallies on the courthouse lawn. After working for a time in Montgomery County, Nazelrod returned to Garrett County and began work as a heavy equipment mechanic for the State Highway Department, a member of AFSCME.

"I learned [from the strike] that if you get enough guys sticking together, you can do anything," he said.

Recognition of an international union brought some of the cultural change Sines and other union opponents feared. The Association had been composed of both managers and workers. Many shared family ties. Their mutuality was largely centered upon their roles maintaining the county's roads.

But after the recognition of AFSCME, some in the hourly workforce identified as members of the U.S. labor movement. They may have lacked some of the cohesiveness and militancy of other union members, like the United Mine Workers. But they came to realize they had more in common with each other and with others doing similar work, inside and outside of Maryland, than with their county commissioners or anti-union local businesses, regardless of family ties or history.

"Solidarity was a word I heard a lot around the house," says Terry Rinker, a former union Ironworker and son of Local 1834 President Leo Rinker. "I remember going out with my father to [support] a coal mine strike with a 55-gallon barrel [to burn wood]," he added.

Rinker remembered his father forming close friendships with a multiracial group of AFSCME members and leaders while attending conventions and meetings.

Looking back on his father's accomplishments, Terry Rinker said the union helped improve job conditions after the strike and might have saved lives, speculating that the cancer that killed his father may have resulted from the cinders he threw from the back of the truck during heavy snows and ice storms before the union insisted on the purchase of modern equipment.

Tom Kelleher, the AFSCME representative and Vietnam

veteran from Baltimore, said, "These guys [road crews] were salt of the earth. We had a solid contract in Garrett County with meaningful language that was flexible, meeting the needs of both workers and the county." Kelleher recalled contract clauses that allowed workers extra time off during hunting season.

Allen Wilhelm, striker Asa Wilhelm's son, was elected president of his local union, District 50 of the United Mine Workers [later the United Steelworkers] at Harbison-Walker refractory in Jennings. The plant supplied brick for the furnaces of steel mills in Pittsburgh and Baltimore. Wilhelm set a record for productivity, wrapping his hands in inner-tube rubber and "throwing" [stacking] 90 tons of still-hot brick on an eight-hour shift.

Looking back at the roads strike, he said, "There's something wrong when people can't sit down at the table and work things out. There's always some middle ground. There's got to be a way to resolve it. If folks on the other side of the table are unreasonable or hard-headed like Ross Sines, you have to stand your ground. I wouldn't cross a picket line or scab anywhere."

"I remember my dad going out on the picket lines every day," said Nancy Bateman Carrico, the daughter of striker James Bateman. Carrico said her dad, who passed away at age 52, was "really proud that he drove the grader," recalling a day when she got in the vehicle and he drove her to school.

Carrico added, "My mother hated the fact that [the strike] had gotten to that point. But she was behind my dad and she went down to Oakland to stand up. My dad was worried about us going out by ourselves because some people threatened the strikers."

To sustain the family during the strike, Carrico noted that her father "always raised a garden. We were thankful that we could rely upon that. A lot of workers had a rough time because they couldn't get credit [at the local grocery]."

She remembered her father coming home with a box of food from the union's distribution center and how she went "into town" after the strike to buy a shirt for her dad to wear to the victory party.

During high school and after graduation, Carrico worked at Garrett Manufacturing Co. When the International Ladies Garment

Workers began organizing a unit at the shirt factory, a supervisor advised her against voting for the union. Carrico asked her father how she should vote. "My dad said, 'Nancy, you need a union behind you.' So, I went ahead and agreed."

James Lininger Jr. said his father, James Lininger Sr., a 10-year employee at the time of the strike, "wasn't what I would call really enthusiastic about the strike." His father had grown up on a farm in Friendsville, today's site of the town park. In 1962, he bought a school bus, contracting with the school system.

"There just weren't job opportunities here," said Lininger. He took a locomotive training course in Tennessee and then, during the strike, worked as a machinist apprentice at Bethlehem Steel's Sparrows Point plant near Baltimore.

Lininger returned to Western Maryland and for 15 years, drove a truck, transporting goods across the country. After the strike, his father quit the roads department and joined his son in business excavating residential sites for homes.

"I don't tow the union line," said Lininger Jr., "but I understand a little bit about their importance. Because we were so rural, the politics didn't catch up [to the more urban areas]."

"The banking and the powers in the county didn't accept a lot of change," said Lininger Jr., who also had great uncles in the Vitez family among the strikers. "The roads strike wasn't as contentious as people may have thought and the strike was one of the catalysts for some of the better things in the county [raising wages]," said Lininger Jr., who sat on the executive committee of the school bus contractor's association and served in the volunteer fire department for 50 years.

Some Garrett County families remained resolutely opposed to unionism. Hugh Friend of Friendsville said, "The strikers were the problem." He recalled his father, Stanton Friend, a farmer, traveling to Oakland with some of his neighbors to support Commissioners Friend and Sines during the battle of the bus. His father, who was related to Hubert Friend, was "just like other farmers who didn't think much of unions.

"A lot of people were happy to work for the county roads department. But the [union] road workers got hateful and combative."

A retired teacher, Friend recalled hearing about the planks

with spikes strikers put under the tires of the bus hired to take strikebreakers to work. And he remembered hearing about Maryland state troopers "just standing there watching" [during the battle of the bus].

"To me, it's amazing the strikers won their case," said Friend. "They didn't have any backing from people in Garrett County."

He continued, "People got tired of not having roads fixed and plowed. They [the citizens] capitulated [to the union]. What else could they do? What can Ford Motor Co. do when the workers go on strike?" asked Friend, still running a 250-acre cattle farm in 2020 at age 83.

During his teaching career in Salisbury, Pennsylvania, Friend joined the teachers' union, but said, "I really didn't want to join." Then he stopped paying dues. "I was ostracized pretty heavy [by other teachers] and started paying dues again," said Friend, who later became president of the Friend Family Association, archiving the family's history in the United States.

In 1975, Frank Vitez, the son of striker James Vitez, helped found HV Testing, located in the Central Garrett County Industrial Park. The company developed into Phenix Technologies, a global producer. Vitez sold the business in 2021.

Stephen Schlosnagle, author of *Garrett County-A History of Maryland's Tableland*, grew up on a dairy farm outside of Accident and was 16 years-old at the time of the strike. Schlosnagle said, "Ideology was very much part of [opposition] to the strike. AFSCME's arrival was to many farmers, like a communist invasion…like they needed to get their pitchforks out. The [attitude] was, 'Our sons are fighting communism in Vietnam, but the communists [unions] are arriving in Garrett County.'"

Schlosnagle added, "The ideological attack on unionism was accompanied by a "long and deep undercurrent of racism" in the county targeting Black unionists who arrived from Baltimore to support the road workers .

Schlosnagle recalls working in the 1990s on restoration of the Drane House, the oldest continuously occupied white settler house in the county, built by slave labor for its tobacco farmer owners. One of the volunteers on the project, pointed to the farm field adjacent to the house and said, "That's where the Ni—ers are buried [in unmarked graves]."

Curtis Nazelrod, the son of striker Eugene Nazelrod said, "Even though the Civil Rights Act had been passed, the county was very prejudiced." His parents rejected racial prejudice and his father's service in WWII helped encourage the elder Nazelrod to tell his children, "We all bleed red."

"I fell in love with Val Wilson," a Black Baltimore City worker who came to the county with AFSCME's caravan. Nazelrod, whose family has "some Cherokee blood," said he regrets losing a photo of Wilson, the "big man in a white shirt and straw cowboy hat" giving him a hug on the county courthouse steps.

"I made lasting friends with the Spiker and Sweitzer kids and others from our time on the picket lines with our daddies," said Curtis Nazelrod. "We hung together during the strike. We were poor kids who couldn't afford fancy clothes and didn't fit in with the rich kids in school. We became friends, not just acquaintances."

Nazelrod said that, "If it wasn't for food stamps and the caravans from Baltimore during the strike, we would have been screwed. I remember catching crawdads and eating them and shooting squirrels before school, leaving them in the cold, and skinning them when I got home."

He recalled helping his father wire houses during the strike and delivering goods to Joe Gower, who owned a local junk shop, for some extra cash. "The strike helped everyone," said Nazelrod. "My aunt Geraldine served as clerk of the court. After the strike, she, too, was represented by the union."

One of the most dramatic cultural changes in the union's wake came several years after the strike. Cathy Lyons, the coal miner's daughter from Kitzmiller and former GCCAC community aide, turned in an application for the roads department. Her husband Clarence Lyons was already working for the roads after a stint at Bethlehem Steel's Sparrows Point plant.

Jim Lyons, Mary's son, said, "I don't know exactly what happened, but she got word they [the county] didn't even look at her application and threw it in a trash can." His mother could run a power saw and drive a truck. "She was tough. She did Skoal (chewing tobacco), fished, loved to hunt turkeys and was a powerful softball player."

Cathy Lyons filed an employment discrimination charge and was soon hired and issued an apology from the Garrett County commissioners for not considering her for the roads crew.

The sole woman in the department, Cathy Lyons applied her skills to running the paver, one of the top jobs on the crew. The men elected her president of Local 1834. AFSCME Council 67 assigned John Gates as the servicing staff representative to work with Lyons on grievances and negotiations.

Gates, a Black native of Cumberland, worked as a backhoe operator for the City of Cumberland, serving as president of AFSCME Local 553. Recalling his first trips to Garrett County, Gates said Local 1834 members held union meetings at the volunteer fire department in McHenry.

"It was their social night out. After the meeting, the men played cards," he said. Staying for the card games, Gates would hear road workers "dropping the 'N' word" during discussions. Lyons assailed any disrespect directed at Gates. "Mary told them, 'He [Gates] is one of us. [a road worker and union member].'"

Lyons and Gates formed a tight team, professionally and socially, with Gates and his brother, a Vietnam veteran, sometimes joining Mary and her husband on fishing trips. "Mary was very tough, very direct and fierce," said Gates, first cousin of Henry Louis Gates, Jr., the Harvard professor and genealogist who grew up in nearby Piedmont, West Virginia, the son of a Luke paper mill worker.

"When people were pushing back, Mary would point her finger and say, 'Once you understand the issue, you will understand why I am taking [a particular] position,'" said Gates.

"My mother didn't like people to be taken advantage of," said Jim Lyons, a retired Teamster member who worked out of the Pepsi distribution center in Cumberland and stocked the shelves at Wal-Mart in Oakland before retiring in 2020.

In 1990, AFSCME held a dinner/dance at Wisp Resort to commemorate the roads strike. John Gates welcomed the attendees and Cathy Lyons delivered remarks. The keynote speaker was AFSCME President Gerald McEntee. Large photos of strikers lined the walls and strikers in attendance were given special recognition.

17

COMMEMORATING THE STRIKE.

"Solidarity is not a matter of sentiment but a fact, cold and impassive as the granite foundations of a skyscraper. If the basic elements, identity of interest, clarity of vision, honesty of intent, and oneness of purpose, or any of these is lacking, all sentimental pleas for solidarity, and all other efforts to achieve it will be barren of results."

- Eugene Debs

In 2014, Saul Schniderman, an AFSCME local president at the Library of Congress in Washington, D.C., suggested the Western Maryland Central Labor Council (AFL-CIO) lobby for a state historical road marker commemorating the roads strike.

Schniderman, a Takoma Park, Maryland resident, had launched his own successful effort to erect a road marker in Silver Spring, Maryland in honor of Mary "Mother" Jones, the legendary United Mine Workers organizer. The sign was dedicated in 2000. No action was taken on Schniderman's roads suggestion until 2019, when Jody Oliver, executive director of the Western Maryland AFL-CIO Central Labor Council, asked the council to endorse a campaign for a state historical marker.

The first letter to the state endorsing the marker came from retired Deputy Sheriff, Orphan's Court judge, Garrett County Commissioner and Republican Central Committee member Wayne Wilt. Wilt, the former director of the state's Juvenile Services Department in Garrett County, was the longest AFSCME dues-payer in the county.

Dozens of letters followed from other county residents, labor unions and labor historians across the state endorsing the road marker. Peter Kurtze, who formerly directed the state's program, said he had never seen so much support for a historic road marker.

In October 2019, the state approved the request. Plans were immediately put in place for a dedication ceremony to be held on April 7, 2020, 50 years after the start of the strike. The plans were delayed due to the COVID 19 pandemic. The sign remained in the State Highway Department's shop in Hanover, Maryland.

Finally, On June 8, 2021, 125 people gathered under a tent outside the administrative offices of the Garrett County Roads Department to dedicate the road marker. AFSCME International Vice President Glenard Middleton, executive director of Council 67, supplied the tent, food, and sound system. Several members of Council 67 accompanied him to the dedication.

More than thirty-five members of the strikers' families showed up. They included Jay Sowers, the son of Local 1834 President Jack Sowers, and Terry Rinker and Mel Rinker Savage, the children of Local 1834 President Calvin "Leo" Rinker. Tom Holler, the son of striker Lyden "Roy" Holler, and Donna Evans, the wife of striker Rodger Evans, helped mobilize families to attend.

Family members brought framed pictures of the strikers and their wives. Rosalee Finch also made phone calls and sent letters to close relatives. Finch was the widow of Deputy Sheriff Frank Finch, whose parents were active in the strike, and the niece of Dominic Pratt, an outspoken union roads worker.

Workers at the Roads Department's Oakland garage, just up the street, brought a wooden picket sign from the strike that still sat atop the bank of lockers in the locker room. The dust-covered sign had been salvaged by Jeff DeWitt, the purchasing agent in the Oakland garage and a nephew of roads strikers, during a move from the county's former garage.

Two road strikers attended the commemoration—Troy Wakefield, hired only a month before the strike, and Paul Cosner, who spent a year in prison, charged with dynamiting Commissioner Hubert Friend's fence. Jeff Friend, former AFSCME Local 1834 President, and son of striker Ernest Friend, was also in attendance.

Western Maryland union leaders showed up, including Mayor Rob Reckart of Kitzmiller, Maryland, a Carpenter's union leader, and Greg Harvey, president of United Steelworkers Local 676 at the former Verso paper mill in Luke, Maryland.

Lynne Elmlinger, former president of the Garrett County Teachers Association, attended the dedication. So did George Koontz, president of International Brotherhood of Electrical Workers Local 307 in Cumberland and president of the Western Maryland Central Labor Council (AFL-CIO).

"As I was listening to the stories at the unveiling, I did find tears welling in my eyes. I'm proud to be union and a Garrett County native," said Reckart.

"Junior" DeWitt, a member of the executive board of AFSCME Local 1834 came to the dedication ceremony on his day off. DeWitt said, "I felt I needed to be there for those who couldn't be, like [striker and later foreman] Sheldon Whitacre [then in a nursing home in Oakland], and Cathy Lyons [former Local 1834 president]."

Influential longtime county residents attended, including Duane Yoder, Smokey Stanton, and Lowell Bender. And the ceremony drew in activists from the Garrett County Democratic Club, leaders of the seven-year successful battle against hydraulic fracturing (fracking) in the county, and members of dozens of county organizations.

Two representatives of the Garrett County Historical Society were present, marking an advance in the group's recognition of the importance of the strike. Two years earlier, the society's board declined to endorse the marker campaign, saying they "would not oppose the effort."

The dedication ceremony drew some unexpected interest from outside the county. Attendees included David Ettlin of Pasadena, Maryland, a retired Baltimore Sun reporter/editor who, on one of his first assignments for the paper, reported on the battle of the bus.

Also present was David Kusnet of Washington, D.C., a former AFSCME communications leader. Kusnet, who wrote speeches for AFSCME President Jerry Wurf, later served as chief speechwriter for former President Bill Clinton.

Ernie "Butch" Crofoot Jr., son of the AFSCME Council 67 leader at the time of the strike, traveled from the Eastern Shore of Maryland to join the commemoration. Butch, then a B&O Railroad worker, played guitar and sang a song by labor troubadour Phil Ochs (1940-1976) on the steps of the Garrett County courthouse during

197

the conflict.

Paul Edwards, president of the Garrett County Board of Commissioners, son of state senator and former commissioner George Edwards, welcomed attendees.

"History defines a place and gives it its character," said Edwards, director of secondary education in Garrett County. "I'm ashamed that during my 10-years as a history teacher, I never learned more about the strike or discussed the strike with my students."

Mayor Don Sincell of Mountain Lake Park, the former publisher of *The Republican,* said, "Unions have gotten a bum rap. The 'bad guys' were the CEOs and employers who abused workers and the 'good guys' were those who organized and stood together to make things better for their co-workers."

Sincell, who has initiated dialogue on the county's racial exclusivity and led efforts to rehabilitate and relocate the county's only Black church for visitors, brought personal recollections affirming the need for unions.

"I worked construction for a summer before starting college. I made $2.25 an hour. But county roads workers, who had families to support, only averaged $1.97 an hour," said, who graduated high school the year of the strike.

Former AFSCME staff representative John Gates recounted the 1990 commemoration of the strike at Wisp Resort he helped organize with former Local 1834 President, Cathy Lyons.

"Cathy was little in stature, but big on commitment," said Gates, who also recognized former Local 1834 President Jeff Friend. "It was Jeff Friend's deep knowledge of the county's people and politics that enabled Local 1834 to sign good contracts and advance the living standards of its members."

Gates paid tribute to Ray Clarke, the deceased president of AFSCME Local 44 who represented municipal workers in Baltimore City and led caravans to Oakland during the strike.

"People in Oakland were buzzing [pro and con] for days" after Clarke and other Black Baltimore brothers, returned home, said Gates, who underscored the close connection between the civil rights movement and the labor movement in the wake of AFSCME's

Memphis Sanitation Strike.

The dedication ceremony was prominently covered in *The Republican* and the *Cumberland Times-News*. Print and social media attention revived memories and invoked new interest in the strike.

Tracie Ellis, the granddaughter of striker and active union member Ernest Friend and niece of former Local 1834 President Jeff Friend, posted on Facebook: "Thank you for making my day. I started scrolling through my newsfeed, paused on this [marker announcement] and now I've been reading everything on the [strike history] website. I knew my Pap [Ernest Friend] was part of this, but I didn't realize how historic this was for our country."

Darla Fay Liller-Bockstanz, the daughter of roads striker Dayton Broadwater, also responded on Facebook: "The strike was very hard on my parents as my mom was pregnant with me. I've been referred to as the 'strike baby' many times. When I was old enough to understand, my parents explained what that meant to me."

THIS BOOK CONTINUES ONLINE!

QR CODE LINK TO WEB SITE

LINK TO WEB SITE:
https://garrettroadstrike.com

The 1970 Road Strike marked a turning point in the economic, cultural and political life of Garrett County.

Duane Yoder, president emeritus, Garrett County Community Action Committee, said, "I can't imagine that change happening without the dramatic change [the strike precipitated]. The homogeneity of Garrett County retards our progress."

Based upon dozens of interviews with longstanding county residents, the online section of this book examines the decade following the strike, the key players in the county's emergence as a tourism and real estate center, and the challenges facing the county's farmers and its working-class majority.

Among the subjects covered are:

* A new wave of outsiders
* Professionalizing county government
* Deep Creek Lake and WISP

* The League of Women Voters
* The Underground Church
* Environmental and Sanitation Struggles
* The "Scenic and Wild River" Battle
* Collective Bargaining in the county
* Bradley Manor and Public Housing Controversies
* Plant Shutdowns
* Northern Garrett County in Transition
* Today's Road Workers

Head to the Garret County Road Strike web site for a rich trove of historical material!

AFTERWORD

I owe so much to the good souls who patiently peeled off some of the mysteries of Garrett County to a former city guy and put me in touch with so many of their friends and neighbors. Thank you, Tom Dabney, Smokey Stanton, Ina Hicks, Lowell Bender, Rosalee Finch, Tom Bernard, Lynne Elmlinger, Duane Yoder, Curtis Nazelrod, Mayor Carolyn Corley, Tim Galica, Mayor Rob Reckart, Steve Schlosnagle, the late Doug Railey, and so many others.

The surviving strikers and their families will forever be in my heart. Every one of them helped reconstruct the story of their struggle, knowing if they didn't tap their memories and contacts, their histories would be buried, along with so many loving peers.

Thank you so much to former deputy sheriff and commissioner Wayne Wilt, who sent the first letter to Garrett County Board of Commissioners President Paul Edwards, and to everyone who helped the state's Historical Trust more fully understand the significance of the events of 1970.

Photos and newspaper clippings played a vital role in helping participants and social media users remember the details and people at the center of this story. Thanks to Stefanie Caloia, AFSCME archivist, Walter P. Reuther library at Wayne State University, and Lisa Zakharova, special collections librarian/archivist at Frostburg State University for their help in accessing documents and photos. Thanks to Mike Bello for covering the road marker unveiling and sharpening up some of the historical photos.

Thanks to John McGowan, Chris Nichols, and other folks at the Garrett County Historical Society who acknowledged a significant lapse in their historical work and invited me to tell the story of the strike in the *Glades Star*.

Al Feldstein, Cumberland's prolific historian, a member of the Maryland Historical Trust, contributed a great photo and encouragement for the project. Lynne Bowman first opened my eyes to the history of slavery and racial exclusion in Mountain Maryland. The history of Black people in Garrett County has been greatly deepened by the work of Karen White, curator of the Garrett County Historical Society, and George Cowgill.

Thanks to Southern High School educator Harry Biggs for taking time to talk about his family's history in the region and for inviting me to address his students about the strike and organized labor. Thanks to Bill Barry for the opportunity to address his labor studies classes.

Thanks to the Garrett County Democratic Central Committee for awarding my work on this project.

Thanks to Don Sincell for making hard copies of *The Republican* available for research, and to the late Mary Sincell McKewin for working with Thomas Vose to digitize back issues.

Thanks to Carol Riley-Alexander, executive assistant, Garrett County Government, for supplying minutes of Board of Commissioners meetings before and during the strike. Any historian reviewing those minutes—so carefully kept by the county's clerks, Virginia Pfizer and Harold Adams—knows how great a decision Carol made years ago to employ a summer intern to scan them and make them easily available.

Thanks to Kim Durst, Garrett County's economic development specialist, for her help researching the history of Sterling Processing.

Thanks to Karen Brewer, administrative assistant to the Superintendent of Schools of Garrett County.

Thanks to Deb Frantz and her brother, Ed Filsinger, Webster Hoover, and Mary Bach for helping pry open the history of some of the men who formed the Garrett County Roads Employees' Association back in 1956.

Thanks to Kara Rogers Thomas for inviting me to exhibit at the Appalachian Festival at Frostburg State University. Thanks also to Theresa Miller, administrative roads coordinator for the Garrett County Roads Department, for helping supply contacts for roads employees and for encouraging this project.

Thanks to Stephen Schlosnagle, whose reassessment of his historical research on Garrett County helps give context to today's efforts to build a more equitable, progressive county.

Thanks to my former co-worker and trusted friend Lucas Oswalt for his tireless work on the strike history website. Thanks to Judy Devlin for keeping the tradition of small-town booksellers alive in Garrett County.

I owe deep gratitude to Rafael Alvarez for his encouragement, his frank advice, humor, and friendship.

Thanks to Paul Roberts, who reviewed this book in its eleventh hour and made a compelling case for constructive changes.

Thanks to Tim Sheard and Hardball Press for your hard work and guidance on this book.

Thanks to everyone I haven't mentioned who contributed to telling this history and honoring the struggle of workers for a voice on the job.

During my writing, as expected, other folks I interviewed passed on. They include Kenna "Joe" Heatherman, Lillian Sines, Monsignor Paul Byrnes, Dwayne Wilhelm, Rodger Evans, Doug Railey, Ray Metz, Troy Wakefield, Gary Friend, Walter Johnson, Paul Cosner, Mary Bach, Herb McCrobie, Ernie Gregg, Rev. Don Matthews, Johnny Tasker, Jim Fike, Sheldon Whitacre, Wayne Johnson.

Ray Metz, retired AFSCME staffer, called me two weeks before his death from cancer to make sure I had his best and last memories of the strike and Garrett County. He so desperately wanted to be at the commemoration. Many who gathered under the tent that day sorely felt his absence.

Finally, thanks most profoundly to Maxine Shindel. She suffered through my three years of rambling about people, places and squabbles, deals made, and deals broken, but still gave wonderfully constructive advice.

Len Shindel
Oakland, Md.
2025

HISTORIC ROAD MARKER SUPPORTERS & INTERVIEW SUBJECTS

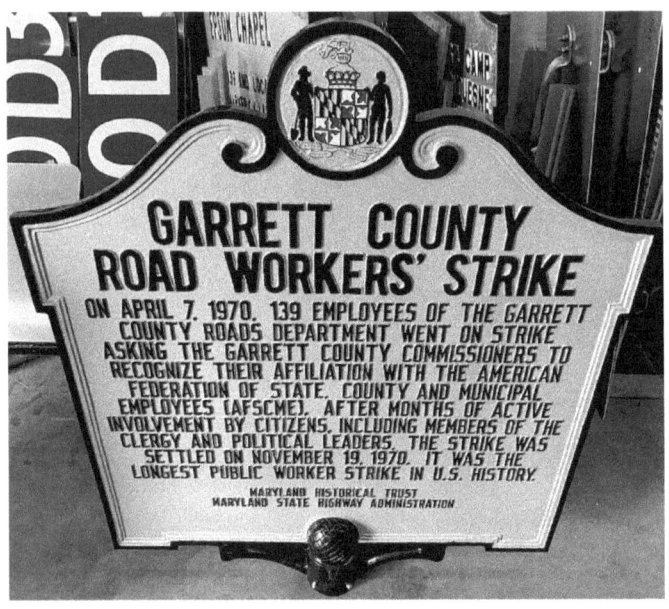

The author wishes to honor those who supported erecting the Historic Road Marker commemorating the Strike of 1970:

Garrett County Board of Commissioners Chairman Paul Edwards; Glennard S. Middleton, AFSCME Council 67; Courtney ("CJ") Jenkins, American Postal Workers Union Local 181; Edward Mohler, president emeritus, Maryland State/DC AFL-CIO; Michael Honey, University of Washington; Dick Carroll, Garrett Institute for Lifelong Learning; Paul Shackel, University of Md.; Jackie Jeter, president, Metro Wash. Council AFL-CIO; Ernest (Billy) Thompson, district director, United Steelworkers District 8; Patrick Hunt, former researcher, Communications Workers of America; Judy Carbone, American Association of University Women; Lowell Bender, retired administrator, Garrett College; Bob and Helen Spear, Prince Georges County educators; Kevin Faley, former U.S. Senate committee counsel; Michael Bell, educator; J. Mark Richards, past president, IAFF Local 2000, Howard County Professional Firefighters; Thomas B. Dabney, Jr., Garrett County attorney; Gene Bruskin, playwright and former union organizer; H. Wayne Wilt, retired Garrett County deputy sheriff and director of Juvenile Services; Bill Barry, Baltimore labor educator; Susan Flashman, president, Maryland/DC Alliance for Retired Americans; Patrick Moran, president, AFSCME Council 3; Saul Schniderman, Labor Heritage Foundation; and any others about whose support I have not been informed.

Interview Subjects:

Bill Aiken, Violet Alexander, Lonnie Artice, Mary Bach, Velma Beckman, Dave and Beverly Beard, Del. Wendell Beitzel, Lowell Bender, Rick Bender, Steven Bender, Tom Bernard, Bennie Beckman, James Beckman, Harry Biggs, Darla Fay Liller-Bockstanz, Janet and Tim Brant, John Braskey, Dorothy Broadwater, Maurice Brookhart, Linda Keller Burch, Msgr. Paul Byrnes, Mabel Butler, Sharon Caple, Nancy Bateman Carrico, Sheila Coleman-Castells, Don "Toby" Colaw, Sheila and Dan Convis, Paul Cosner, Ernie Chris Crabtree, "Butch" Crofoot Jr., Dayle Dabney, Sandra Denton, Joe DeSimone, Junior DeWitt, Vera Dunithan, Tom Doyle, Tim Dugan, Paul Durham, State Sen. George Edwards, County Commission Chairman Paul C. Edwards, Betty Elliott, Tracie Ellis, Barbara Englander, Bob Enten, Rodger and Donna Evans, Msgr. Martin Field, Rosalie Finch, Todd Glover, David Ettlin, Heidi Fazenbaker, Buck Fike, Jim and Helen Fike, Rosalie Finch, Ed Filsinger, Helen Fitzwater, Mark Folk, Deb Frantz, Mary Frazee, Edwin Friend, Hugh Friend, Jeff and Gary Friend, Tim Galica, John Gates, Bob Gatto, Tom Gearhart, Joyce Gladhill, Rodney Glotfelty, Todd Glover, Jeremy Gosnell, Leigh Sylvester Graham, Ernie Gregg, Ginny Grove, Bill and Diana Guthrie, Edgar Harman, Freddie Harrison, Charley Harvey, Willard "Bill" Hawkins, Joe Heatherman, Gail and Steve Herman, Norma Hesen, Ina Hicks, Pete Hoefer, Tom Holler, Webster Hoover, T.R. Janes, Victoria Johnson, Wayne Johnson, Phil Jones, Tom Kelleher, Janet Tasker Keller, Mary King, Jennifer Yell Kirwin, Bill Klotz,

Allen Knotts, Ann Leighton, Andy Lewis, Elbert Lewis, Shirley Lewis, Billy Lindner, James Lininger, Dale Lipscomb, Harold Junior Lowdermilk, Jeff Lyons, James Margroff, Johnny and Elaine Marple, Willetta Mateer Rev. Don Matthews, Ray Mattingly, Harold Maust, Ray Metz, Herb McCrobie, Josh McKnight, Noreen Mellick, Leo Miller, Mary Miltenberger, Ed Mohler, Kathleen Moors, Michael Naylor, Curtis Nazelrod, John Nazelrod, Victor Nazelrod, John Nelson, Pam Nelson, Luther Parrack, Carroll Paugh, Shelby Paugh, Fred Pratt, Paul Pratt, Betty Pritt, Tammy Nazelrod Pritt, Jim Raley, Dave and Sara Ramsey, Doris Ray, Theodore Raynovich Jr., Marshall Rickert, Terry Rinker, Keith Roberts, Beverly Railey Robinson, Pastor Scott Robinson, Bob Rudy, Jerry Sanders, Cinda Savage, Stephen Schlosnagle, Ralph Schmidt, Rev. Richard Seaks, Rick Selders, Frank Shap, Renee Shreve, David Sines, Ross and Marie Sines, Lillian Sines, Kate Smith, Kathie Smith, Rob Smith, James Spear, Lance Spiker, Robin Spiker, Alice Stevens, Bonnie Swyter, Helen Tasker, Johnny Tasker, Rev. Daryl Tichinel, Charles Tranum, Vondell Troutman, Jim Umbrell, Thomas Van Meter, Frank Vitez, Troy Wakefield, Patty Wells, Lillian Wertz, Shari Riggleman Whetstone, Sheldon and Nadean Whitacre, Jesse Whittemore, Chris Wildesen, Allen Wilhelm, Dwayne Wilhelm, Becky Hamilton Wilkerson, Wayne Wilt and Duane Yoder.

BIBLIOGRAPHY

Billings, Richard N., John Greenya, <u>Power to the Public Worker</u>. Washington-New York: Robert B. Luce Inc., 1974

Bowman, Lynn, <u>Everyone Counts-A History of African American Enslavement in Allegany County, Maryland</u>. (self-published) Frostburg, Md., 2018

Cowgill, George, <u>Another Visit to the Mountaintop-A History of Mountain Lake Park, Maryland 1881-1921.</u> Columbia, SC: Big Pasture Publishing, LLC, 2023

Estep, William R., <u>The Anabaptist Story-An Introduction to Sixteenth-Century Anabaptism</u>. Grand Rapids: William B. Eerdmans Publishing Co., 1996

Foner, Philip S., <u>The Great Labor Uprising of 1877</u>. New York: Pathfinder, 1977

Goulden, Joseph C., <u>Jerry Wurf: Labor's Last Angry Man</u>. New York: Atheneum, 1982

Harvey, Katherine A., <u>The Best-Dressed Miners-Life and Labor in the Maryland Coal Region-1835-1910</u>. Ithaca: Cornell University Press, 1969

Hattery, Thomas H., ed., <u>Western Maryland: A Profile</u>. Mt. Airy, Md.: Lomond Books, 1980

Jewell, Katherine Rye, <u>Dollars for Dixie-Business and the Transformation of Conservatism in the Twentieth Century</u>. Sheridan Books, 2017

Kramer, Leo, <u>Labor's Paradox-The American Federation of State, County, and Municipal Employees AFL-CIO</u>. New York: John Wiley and Sons, Inc., 1962

Matthews, Donald, <u>The Journey of a Country Preacher</u>. Oakland, Md.: DiggyPOD, 2017

Meyer, Eugene L., <u>Maryland Lost and Found Again</u>. Centreville, Md: Tidewater Publishers, 1986

Nordin, D. Sven, Rich Harvest-A History of the Grange, 1867-1900. Jackson: University of Mississippi Press, 1974

Orleck, Annelise, Lisa Hazirjian, eds., The War on Poverty. Athens: University of Georgia Press, 2011

Rada Jr., James, Saving Shallmar-Christmas Spirit in a Coal Town. Gettysburg: Legacy Publishing, 2012

Rascovar, Barry, The Great Game of Maryland Politics. Baltimore: Baltimore Sun, 1998

Ryan, Francis, AFSCME'S Philadelphia Story-Municipal Workers and Urban Power in theTwentieth Century. Philadelphia: Temple University Press, 2011

Shaffer, Robert C., History of Crellin, Maryland-Story of a Double Boom Town. Oakland, Md.: Sincell Publishing Company, 1976

Slater, Joseph E., Public Workers-Government Employee Unions, the Law, and the State 1900-1962. Ithaca: Cornell University Press, 2004.

Smith, Herbert C., John T. Willis, Maryland Politics and Government-Democratic Dominance. Lincoln: University of Nebraska Press, 2012

Spero, Sterling, Government As Employer. New York: Remsen Press, 1948

Windham, Lane, Knocking on Labor's Door-Union Organizing in the 1970s and the Roots of a New Economic Divide. Chapel Hill: University of North Carolina Press, 2017

Online

Garrett College, Indigenous Peoples of Garrett County, https://garrettcollege.libguides.com/gcindigenouspeoples/home
Western Maryland's Historical Library, www.whilbr.org

LIST OF STRIKERS

OAKLAND GARAGE

Baker, Clark

Bateman, Charles

Bateman, James

Blamble, Frank

Bowser, Frederick

Brant, Harold

Colaw, Don R.

Collings, Darby

DeWitt, David

DeWitt, Harold C.

Ellifritz, Ellis

Evans, Rodger

Fike, Wayne

Finch, William

Freeland, Delwood

Friend, Albert

Friend, Harvey

Friend, LeRoy

Fries, Arlie

George, A. Fred

Guthrie, LeRoy

Holler, James L.

Humberson, Glenn

Keefer, Howard

King, Harry

Knotts, Theodore

Landis, Harold

Lewis, Henry

Lewis, Oliver

Lewis, Stanley

Lowdermlk, Charles

Lowdermilk, Harold J.

Nazelrod, Victor

Pratt, Dominic

Riggleman, Harold

Roth, Howard

Savage, Robert E.
Shaffer, C.D.
Shreve, Salem Jr.
Sowers, Jack
Spiker, Thomas
Stephens, James
Sweitzer, J.D.
Tichnell, Martin
Trickett, Henry
Welch, Clarence
Welch, Cecil
Whitacre, Joseph
White, George F.
Bowmer, Clarence

Fike, James
Filsinger, John
Holler, Lyden
Martin, Foster
Nally, Bernard
Peck, Jonas
Savage, Stanley
Steyer, Ronald
Tasker, Johnny
Wood, Stanley
Glover, Richard
Simms, Sheridan
Whitacre, Sheldon

ACCIDENT GARAGE

Artice, Ray
Fike, Claude
Frantz, Glenn
Frazee, Clement
Frazee, Floyd
Friend, Charles
Griffith, Harry
Hetrick, Earl
Kelso, Lester

King, Richard
Lewis, Lawrence
Metheny, Edward
Rinker, Calvin
Thomas, Paul
Uphold, Danny
Vitez, George
Fazenbaker, Jonas L.

SANG RUN QUARRY

Carr, Charles Jr.
Carr, Charlie Reed
Carr, Thomas
Cosner, Paul W. Jr.
Cuppett, Claude
DeWitt, Emory
DeWitt, George
Friend, David C.
Friend, David Lee
Friend, Ernest

Friend, Everett
Friend, James
Glotfelty, Richard
Haenftling, Leonard
McCrobie, Joseph
Ringer, Charles
Savage Elwood
Savage, Marlin
Wakefield, Troy

212

GRANTSVILLE GARAGE

Atwood, Hollie
Bittinger, John
Bittinger, Lester O
Broadwater, Alonzo
Broadwater, Dayton
Butler, Berman
Chaney, Lawrence
Colmer, Paul E.
Fadeley, James
Fike, Harold
Friend, John M.
Garlitz, Charles
Garlitz, Earl
Garlitz, Roy

Glotfelty, Homer
Guard, John J.
Guthrie, Harvey
Lininger, James
Miller, Leo
McKenzie, Ralph
McKenzie, Regis
Turner, Charles
Vitez, James
Weimer, Ronald
Wilbur, Claude W.
Wilhelm, Asa
Wilhelm, Ray
Wilt, Rob

MORE TITLES FROM HARD BALL PRESS

www.ingramcontent.com/pod-product-compliance
Lightning Source LLC
Chambersburg PA
CBHW050446150626
46551CB00029B/1808